This Could Be You

Destiny Christian Center

Copyright © 2007 Good Catch Publishing, Beaverton, OR.

All rights reserved. Written permission must be secured from the publisher to use or reproduce any part of this book, except for brief quotations in critical reviews or articles.

This book was written for the express purpose of conveying the love and mercy of Jesus Christ. The statements in this book are substantially true; however, names and minor details have been changed to protect people and situations from accusation or incrimination.

All Scripture quotations, unless otherwise noted, are taken from the New International Version Copyright 1973, 1987, 1984 by International Bible Society.

Published in Beaverton, Oregon, by Good Catch Publishing.
www.goodcatchpublishing.com
V1.1

Printed in the United States of America

Table of Contents

	Acknowledgements	9
	Introduction	13
1	Fear Is Not My Destiny	15
2	The Bondage Stops Here	33
3	Power Source	49
4	A Letter To Jennifer	67
5	Steadfast Love	85
6	The Story Of Laura	115
7	Second Chance Drifter	129
	Conclusion	149

Acknowledgements

A book of this nature does not come together without the efforts of a great number of people. We especially want to thank Pastor Bill Bates for his vision to tell the story of these remarkable people. We are so proud of our Good Catch Publishing writers, Amanda Lawrence, Angela Prusia, Peggy Thompson, Jennifer King, Toni Harvey and Rick Drebert. Without your skills, this book would not have the impact it does. For our Good Catch Publishing Project Manager, Julie Penn, who oversaw all of the details, edited and had the responsibility to see the book to completion, we are deeply grateful. Thank you to Violet Angove and Amy Lash who worked diligently from beginning to end with everyone to make the process seamless. A book is often judged by its cover, and we are so happy with the work Evan Earwicker did on the cover. It looks splendid! Finally, to the brave people of Destiny Christian Center who either told or were willing to tell their remarkable stories. They are brave and amazing people, whether their story was used in this book or not.

Daren Lindley
President of Good Catch Publishing

The book you are about to read is a compilation of authentic life stories.
All the facts are true, all the events are real.
These storytellers have dealt with crisis, tragedy, abuse and neglect and have shared their most private moments, mess-ups and hang-ups in order for others to learn and grow from them.
In order to protect the identities of those involved in their pasts, the names of some storytellers have been withheld or changed.

Introduction

Greetings! Everyone loves to win. Win the game; win the argument; win the lottery. Whatever it is, the objective is to always win. When was the last time you knew of someone who struck out on an endeavor just waiting to lose? You see, with winning comes a trophy, a prize, or something that makes the battle worth it, not to mention the prestige that usually accompanies the victory. However, usually the victories cost something. The training, the disciplines, the perseverance, and yes, even the lottery tickets are not free. This book is a collection of stories of people like you and me who are winners, and they are winners because the price for winning had already been paid. They are winners because they are not allowing their past to define them because it is just that, the past — it's over. Their past is also not dictating their future because they have found new hope and new dreams, regardless of their past.

Sincerely,
Bill G. Bates

Fear Is Not My Destiny
The Story of Jen Watson
Written by Jennifer King

I rolled over in my bed as someone gently tousled my hair. I expected to see my mom or dad whispering goodnight. My eyes widened as a crazed face stared back.

"Do you know who I am?" he slurred.

"No, I don't," I mumbled and shook my head. Goosebumps spread across my head where he had touched me. Hair on my arms stood up straight like soldiers at attention. My thoughts jumbled. *Why is this strange man in my bedroom in the middle of the night? Who is he? What did he want? How did he get into our house?* A scream began to surface. The stranger reeked of alcohol and smoke. Then, he placed a butcher knife in front of my face. I gasped, letting out a feeble scream. Chills gripped my body.

"Get out of bed. Come on. We're going, we're going. Shut up," he slurred again in a hushed voice. The stranger grabbed hold of my waist and pulled me from the warmth of my blankets. As he held the knife to my head, I shivered.

At the top of the stairs, my older brother, Josh, called from the door of our divided room. "Jen, you okay? Is someone there?"

I had felt sick earlier that night, maybe from the carnival rides or junk food I had eaten. Josh thankfully left the door between our rooms open, in case I needed him.

This Could Be You

"Tell him you're okay. Tell him it's your parents. I have a knife, and I'll kill you," the stranger said through clenched teeth. He staggered as he dragged me down the steps, clutching the knife to my throat.

"I'm fine. Go back to bed. It's okay," I lied to Josh in a high-pitched voice.

I knew Josh could hear the man. The stranger seemed drunk and high and spoke louder than he intended. I shuddered, thinking if the door between the rooms had been closed, my brother might not have heard the man in my room. Glancing at our parents' closed bedroom door, my heart sank. They probably didn't hear the scuffle going on. I went limp and let my feet drag.

"Hurry up, or I'm going to kill you. Let's go. Let's go. Shut up. Stop screaming, and stop crying, or I'll kill you," the man hissed in my ear. He became mad and aggravated as he tried to retrace his steps to exit the house. Lost in the hall, he seethed, "You need to tell me how to get out of here."

I gasped again for air and clawed at the stranger's arms. His plan to take me away from my home hit like a baseball bat. I screamed louder. My brother's voice echoed in my ears while we were heading out our sliding glass door.

"Dad! Mom! Someone's taking Jennifer! Dad! Mom! Wake up!" Josh bellowed, flying down the hall to fling open our parents' bedroom door.

Outside, I tried to wake the neighbors with piercing screams. I hoped to wake the entire neighborhood. I lived in a gated community, and the homes had been built close together. Someone had to hear

Fear Is Not My Destiny

my cries for help. The man pulled me into a grassy area further away from the house. I became hysterical. *Someone please wake up. Please!*

Awake from my screams and Josh's yelling, my dad dashed downstairs from his bed. My mother hurried after him. She checked on Josh and my older sister, Deeanna, while she glanced around for me. "What's going on?"

"Stop!" my dad bellowed at the man kidnapping me.

The stranger whirled around, clutching my waist.

"Stay where you are, or I'm going to kill her!" He held me tighter and placed the knife along my head.

My dad charged at the stranger, knocking him off balance. "Well, you're going to have to kill me first!"

The knife only nicked the side of my head. Dad saved me from a severe stab wound. Seizing the opportunity, I elbowed the man and raced back toward my home.

Upstairs and unaware of the situation, my sister, Deeanna, called the police. "I don't know what's going on outside our house, but I think two men are fighting, maybe in our driveway. I don't know. I think you need to come over here, quick!"

Dad fought the man for control of the knife on the grass outside. The man stabbed my dad's hand a couple times. Ignoring his injuries, Dad continued to restrain the man and fought for our safety. Having a much larger build gave my dad an advantage, and he overtook the man. My dad hit him over and over.

I barged into the house screaming, "He's going to kill me! He's going to kill me!" I slammed into my

This Could Be You

mother at the bottom of the stairs.

"What's going on, Jen?" said my mother. "You're okay. I won't let him hurt you. No one is going to hurt you." She held me tight for a moment and then leapt to the doorway to observe the fight. "Stop! Stop, Ken!" she pleaded with her husband. "He's not conscious, he can't hurt anyone anymore."

Sirens squealed in the distance. The police apprehended the man. He had to be taken away in an ambulance. The police commended my dad for his heroic deed.

"You did the right thing. You were protecting your family," the policeman said, patting my dad on the back. "Don't worry, he's going to live."

***

I sat stunned, unable to move. Earlier that night, I had attended a school carnival, played with my friends and made plans for my 10th birthday party in four days. Now, everything changed. I didn't want to do anything. My mother cradled me in her arms. I never wanted to leave their security.

The local news team arrived on the scene, and my mother knew the story would be aired first thing in the morning. She called several relatives and friends to let them know what had happened in advance.

"Mom, I need to tell you that we had an incident here tonight. A man tried to kidnap Jennifer from our home. He took Jennifer from our house..." my mother stopped to hold back tears.

Fear Is Not My Destiny

"We knew something happened. Your sister-in-law is here. She came over, feeling the need to pray. We have been praying all night, right up to this phone call, for Jennifer's safety," my grandmother said.

Stunned, but not surprised, my mother sat down.

Earlier that night across town, my aunt had awakened around midnight with an incredible urge to pray. She felt led to pray fervently for my safety and security. She drove to her mother's house, and they prayed repeatedly. Not understanding why God had woken her, my aunt obeyed without questions.

The media pounced on the story. The phone in our home rang continuously. Invitations to appear on local news programs and talk shows filled the answering machine and mailbox. A week earlier, another 9-year-old girl had been kidnapped and killed. Everyone wanted my story of how I survived the kidnapping. Media frenzy grew rampant over the fact that I'd escaped from my captor. My dad also became a local hero. I wanted to forget the nightmare, not share it with the whole world. My parents refused to allow me, or our family, to be overexposed by the media. They agreed to only one magazine article. They wanted to protect me from the stress of the kidnapping and try to make life as normal as possible again.

This Could Be You

***

Two weeks later, I mustered up the courage to go to the store with my mother for camera film. She stayed within centimeters of my side. I stuck to her like peanut butter on bread. Cautiously, I scanned the crowds of people. When my mother stepped away for one second, a deranged woman grabbed my arm.

"I'm going to kill you. I'm going to kill you. How dare you..." screamed the homeless woman.

"Ah! Mom, help!" I yelled. *How is this happening again? Who is this crazy woman? Please, someone help!*

Instantly, my mother swooped me up and pushed the woman away. I sobbed into my mother's arms. The store manager called the police, and they arrested the woman. The police explained she was a delusional homeless woman who suffered from mental problems. The whole scene threw me into a fit of fear and helplessness. I swore I'd never leave the house again, ever!

After spending months at the grueling trial for the man that kidnapped me, the court appointed my family a counselor. My mind was muddled and confused. The fear of the kidnapper coming back consumed my thoughts. The vision of the man's anger, his smell and the knife stayed programmed in my mind like a horror movie. His face and his hair flashed in my thoughts. I believed he'd find me again and succeed in taking me away. As I tried again to venture out with my mother, fear gripped my body. Heart pounding, I squealed when a man

Fear Is Not My Destiny

looked my way. "Mom! Mom! I think that's him! It's the man who took me!"

"No, honey. He's in prison. He went to jail. He's going to be in prison a long time. You don't have to worry," my mother said, securing an arm around my shoulder for comfort.

Fear prevented me from venturing outside to play during the summer. I didn't go outside at all. Eventually, I stopped taking dance lessons or attending brownie meetings. Paralyzed with fear, I sat home every day. I quit my extracurricular activities and began to watch television nonstop. Food filling my lap, I'd stare at the television screen and eat. That summer, I gained a lot of weight while my fear continued to escalate. I tried sleeping in my own room, but fear flooded my thoughts. I'd tremble at rattling windows and creaky floors. The noises in the night quickly sent my feet scrambling down the hall to my parents' bedroom, shaking. My parents had tried everything to comfort me. My counselor had suggested remodeling my bedroom. My family agreed. I completely redecorated my bedroom with new colors, new bedding and new curtains. Sometimes I'd start to go to sleep in my room but ended up in my parents' room within the hour. Each night, I made a makeshift bed on the floor next to my parents' bed. When fear simmered to a boiling point, I'd jump off the floor and cuddle up with them in their bed. Closing my eyes, I waited for the fear to leave. It never did for six years. At 17 years old, I couldn't stay home alone.

"I'm going out for a quick trip to the store. Do

This Could Be You

you want to come?" my mother asked.

Before she finished the question, I grabbed my jacket and followed closely on the heels of my mother heading out the door. I tried to stay home many times, but fear would invade my thoughts and win the battle. A year later, at almost 11 years old, I no longer wanted to see my counselor. I needed to try to forget that terrible night and get on with my life. Reliving the kidnapping through talking over and over only caused frustration. Fear plagued my life.

One afternoon, I struggled to stay home alone. Hearing creaking noises from the bedrooms upstairs, I imagined the strange man had broken into our home to find me. The noises grew louder and louder. I felt overcome with the urge to flee and headed out of the house to the packed community pool area. Fear chased me to the pool, and I began obsessing about the man who had tried to kidnap me. Every man at the pool became a kidnapper. I felt sure he'd find me and snatch me up while holding a knife. Being kidnapped again wracked my thoughts. I raced back to our house and sat on the porch, waiting for my mother's return. I suspiciously eyed every car that drove by. Afraid to enter, I stared at my house. I had nowhere else to go. Nowhere to run. Sitting with my back straight up, I peered down the street. I held my breath until my mother's car appeared in the distance. A wave of relief rushed over my body.

In a junior high English class, my teacher read an Edgar Allen Poe story titled, *The Raven*. The dark wording of the poem and the violent nature sent me

Fear Is Not My Destiny

into flashbacks of the kidnapping. I went to the office, where my parents hurried to my side and took me home for the day.

By my junior year in high school, I became withdrawn and shy. I rarely went out with friends or went to their homes. I tried sleepovers a few times but always called my mother, crying for her to come pick me up. Horror movies were popular, and I wanted no part of them. Guys at school made me uncomfortable. I'd rather be at home in the safety of my parents' presence. My mother and older sister became my best friends. They took me everywhere with them and stayed home many nights to comfort me when I felt vulnerable. My sister, Deeanna, changed her plans of moving away to college and went to a local university. This allowed Deeanna freedom to come home and stay with me whenever I needed a shoulder. Deeanna became like a second mother, guarding and protecting me with her heart and soul. I stayed over at Deeanna's apartment on the nights my parents went out.

Years of torment from fear took a toll on my life. I became angry that fear clung to my back like an old coat. I steamed with anger at God for letting bad things happen to good people. To make matters worse, my family faced financial difficulties, and they were about to lose their home. My face flushed. My body felt a surge of fear penetrate every limb.

I cried, "God, if you don't care about me, I'm not going to care about you, either. How could you let my family lose our home?"

During my last few years in high school, I turned

This Could Be You

to alcohol and drugs to numb the fear and pain. I relied on them to help me forget the past and temporarily erase the fear. Going out to drink masked my fear, and I could leave my house. Masking the fear made it easier to be out in the world. Otherwise, my thoughts drove me insane. My sudden and erratic change in behavior shocked my parents. They tried talking to me, but I went from staying home every minute to partying late into the night. My life spiraled downward. Anger became a twin to the fear in my mind. My parents feared the drastic change they witnessed in me. My disbelief in God and my anger toward him became apparent. Getting into trouble became routine, and I hung out with the wrong people. Two new students my senior year in high school brought new adventures. I drank excessively with them until I passed out. The more I drank and dabbled in drugs, the more I began to argue with my mother. I'd argue about anything. Nothing mattered. I opened up to being around guys. I dated many and became sexually active.

My parents losing our home was the last straw with God. After graduation from high school, I went to live with my grandparents while my parents worked on financial issues. My brother and sister were in college, and my parents felt living with our grandparents might encourage me to find hope again. My grandfather was a pastor at a church, and he prayed the positive environment might impact my life. I admired my grandfather and loved him deeply, however, I didn't want religion crammed down my throat. I loved watching my grandparents

Fear Is Not My Destiny

minister to members of their church. They showed great love to everyone, but God wasn't for me.

I felt drained and empty. There had to be more to life than trying to outrun fear or drown fear in a bottle of alcohol. I had even tried erasing the fear by smoking weed. The temporary fixes only worked until the next morning, when fear reared its ugly head again. As the year passed, I became lost. I worked a variety of jobs. None were satisfying. I took a job as a nanny to help out a friend's sister. They paid me well, and I could be back with my old friends to party. It meant leaving my grandparents, but I needed to live on my own.

I continued to drink myself to sleep. On Sundays, I still ventured to local churches. I'd be stinking drunk the night before and sit in church with a hangover. Growing up, my family had always attended church. It was something I'd done my whole life, but my fear issues made me fuming mad at God every time I attended a service.

Partying with friends one night, I passed out in the backseat. Later, I woke up in the middle of the street. I vaguely remembered hearing my friends fighting and pushing me out of the car. I had no clue where I was. Not knowing what to do, I walked to a nearby store and called my brother to pick me up.

"Jen, this isn't safe. This isn't good," Josh said. "You can't be doing this."

I lied about what really happened. My brother saw right through my antics and encouraged me to seek help and change. Back at the nanny house, the 10-year-old girl I took care of had waited up for me.

This Could Be You

"What are you doing up?" I asked.

"Mommy had a party, and she let my brother drink, and he got drunk," said the little girl, giggling.

I sat horrified. Her brother was only 5 years old. I knew right then that this lifestyle wasn't right, and I needed to leave. I called my parents.

"Can you come and get me? I'm living in a really bad environment. I need to leave now. I need to get out," I blubbered into the phone.

"Yes, sweetheart, absolutely. We're on our way," my mother said.

Once back home at my grandparents' house, I tried to give up the partying lifestyle. My family had trouble discussing the issues bothering me. I dated a guy who introduced me to crank and other drugs. I wanted to kill the fear in my body. For two years, I went from guy to guy to guy. I felt like trash. I felt worthless. Deep in my heart, I knew it wasn't right. I was sick of guys walking all over me and sick of my life being in shambles. Finally, at 21 years old, I'd had enough. My grandfather invited me to church to listen to a special sermon from a guest speaker. I drove to the church in anger.

Before entering the church, I prayed, "God, if you're real and you really care about me, you will do something to show me, or I just might end my life."

I trudged into my grandfather's church. The sermon started out normal. The guest speaker held the attention of all with his speech. In the middle of his sermon, the preacher stopped. He made eye contact with me and nodded. Then he shared information

Fear Is Not My Destiny

about my life only God could know.

He's telling my story in front of the whole church, I thought, staring blankly. *He knows everything. He's talking to me. To me! I didn't tell anyone those things.*

I shifted in my seat and looked around the room. Shocked by his words, I shuttered. His tone didn't condemn but showed love. My thoughts raced. *How did he know the details of my hurt and pain? God had heard me. He's using this man to tell my story. He's saying things only God knows.*

The speaker asked me to come forward so he could pray for me. At God's urging, I slowly walked to the front of the church. My knees wobbled. It seemed like the speaker stood a million miles away. Sweat trickled down my back. Heat flushed into my face. The guest speaker started praying over me by laying his hands on my head. He requested healing in the name of Jesus. I felt heat rush from my head to my toes. In a blur, I fell backward and immediately felt God's presence. It felt like a warm blanket had been placed around my shoulders. Silently, I asked God to forgive my sins. My tears were healing and seemed to wash away my pain. At that moment, I knew my journey to escape the grip of fear had started.

For the next few months, I dove into church life. At least, the best I knew how. I often questioned people in the church for help. I continued to struggle with using alcohol to get to sleep at night. It had become my security blanket. I attended classes at my grandfather's church to let go of alcohol. I soaked up the information like a sponge. Each day, I took a step

This Could Be You

closer to understanding God's greatness. I asked many questions to make sure I followed the right path — God's path. Slowly, I gained more confidence in my ability to understand God and his plan for my life.

Eventually, my grandfather retired from their church and moved to Texas. Now, I needed to move on, too. It took only a few weeks to leave my full-time job as senior analyst for a computer company to follow God's leading. The high-paying job didn't matter. I had been called to a higher purpose. The minute I walked into the door of Destiny Church, I knew I belonged here.

God murmured to me, "This is your new home. This is where you're supposed to be."

Years later, at my grandmother's funeral, I sat with my aunt who had prayed for my safety the night I was kidnapped.

"You know, Aunt Melva, the weirdest thing used to happen to me. I used to think I was crazy because I'd be home, and I'd hear voices and other weird things. I'd run out of the house screaming and crying because I thought someone was going to get me," I shared.

My aunt laughed.

"What are you laughing about?" I said.

"I wondered when you were going to talk about this. Every time I came over to your house to visit, I felt an evil presence in your room. Whenever I'd spend the night, I would secretly pray over your room. I even anointed your bed. I'd pray to cast out demons in your room." My aunt smiled at me.

Fear Is Not My Destiny

An evil presence? Anointed? What is she talking about? What does that mean? Am I possessed? I stared at her.

Back at my apartment, I shared what my aunt had said about the spiritual realm to my new Christian friends. "It kind of freaked me out. What is my aunt talking about?" I said.

"Well, let's pray to cast out fear and any evil around you," one of my friends suggested.

"Sounds good to me," I answered, reaching for their hands.

We grasped hands and began to pray. As new Christians, we fumbled for the proper words but continued to pray in God's confidence.

BAM!

"What was that?" we chimed and looked at the dining room table.

The water in my vase of sunflowers turned blood red.

"I'm being choked! I'm being choked! I can't breath!" my friend, Audrey, shrieked, grabbing her neck and struggling for air.

"Start praying. Speak in tongues, do anything!" Jennifer's friend, Laura, screamed, looking at Audrey gasp for air.

Laura and I prayed out loud. We weren't sure what to pray but believed God would speak through us. Laura took leadership over the prayer and started quoting scripture.

"Keep praying, Jennifer. Keep your eyes closed, and keep praying!" Laura yelled over the commotion.

This Could Be You

The old-fashioned window blinds in the apartment flipped open and shut. Then silence. Three minutes passed, but it felt like three hours. I threw the flower-filled vase over the balcony of my apartment into a nearby lake. My friends hugged each other and cried.

"Oh my gosh, was I possessed by a demon? What is going on?" I said. "I'm going to call my mother."

"Honey, I don't believe you were possessed," my mother said over the phone, "but sometimes an evil spirit can attach itself to a person. Like the spirit of fear, but it can be cast off."

"What? What are you talking about?" I questioned.

"Here are some things to pray. Write them down," my mother said and recited a few prayers.

Freaked out and scared at one in the morning, we called a friend. His father was a pastor and told us to pray the blood of Jesus over my life. I had never heard of praying for such things. They were so weird, but I believed in what had happened. My friends and I desperately prayed for fear to be removed from my life.

The next morning, I woke to a sense of peace I had never felt before. I knew the minute I opened my eyes that fear no longer controlled my life. The spirit of fear had left. I felt lighter. Trust in God restored my faith and cast out fear. Fear itself became a lie from the devil. Relieved I had conquered the fear that had plagued my life since I was 9 years old, my heart soared. The world seemed less scary. Excitement rushed through my body. Seeing the world

Fear Is Not My Destiny

without fear was a new and thrilling experience.

12 years later, I cradle my beautiful newborn baby and smile at my older son and stepdaughter. My husband and I worship and praise God together in love. God's miraculous healing power and love has blessed me with a peace beyond all human understanding.

The Bondage Stops Here
The Story of Phyllis
Written by Toni Harvey

"No, Daddy! You're hurting him! Stop it, Daddy! Stop it!"

I came running as I heard the screams of my tiny daughter. She was less than 3 years old at the time.

What I saw when I reached her mortified me. My husband had my youngest son on the bed. "What's wrong with you? Can't you do anything right?" The verbal abuse flowed out of his mouth like molten lava, destroying everything in its path. In this case, it was the fragile spirit of my precious child. He was holding him down, overpowering him, so he couldn't get away. He held his hand tight over his mouth to quiet his screams.

I joined my daughter in pleading for him to stop. He was in such a rage, he didn't even hear us. I don't think he even realized we were in the room. Suddenly, everything blurred. I felt powerless to stop what was happening. All I could do was scoop up my daughter and carry her away to another room so she would not have to witness the abuse inflicted on her half brother by her very own father.

As I closed the door, shutting us into safety, the memories came flooding back. I fell to my knees and started sobbing. I cupped my hands over my ears to stifle the screams and the sounds of the verbal and physical attack I was hearing. It was not only the sounds coming from the next room that I was trying

This Could Be You

to suppress, but it was also the sounds of my past.

* * *

"Stop it! Get away from me!" I yelled at my stepdad, as he chased me from the living room, around the dining room chairs and into the kitchen.

"You worthless, no-good…"

He was angry this time because I hadn't finished my chores for the day. I managed to yank the kitchen door open and flee outside. I stumbled down the steps and out to the road. I paused long enough to scoop up a handful of acorns and throw them back at this abusive man who made every day of my life a living hell.

He saw what I intended to do, so just as I released my handful of acorns, he reached down and took hold of a rock that measured about the size of his fist. Although I had grown accustomed to his daily abuse, there was still a part of me that didn't believe a grown man would intentionally hurt a child my age. I was 13 at the time.

I was foolish to believe, even for a split-second, that this man could demonstrate any amount of grace to another human being. I screamed as I watched the rock sail from his grip through the air and ultimately crash hard into my eye. Blood began streaming down my face. The open gash was just above my right eye, and I had to hold it with my hand as I ran to the neighbor's house. The neighbors weren't home, but I sat on their back steps, sobbing and waiting for what seemed like hours for my mom

The Bondage Stops Here

to get home from work.

My mom had been married to my stepfather for seven years at the time and had grown accustomed to his behavior, but she always tried to protect him. When she finally arrived, she loaded me in the car and took off for the hospital.

As I held my eye and watched the houses and trees outside pass in a blur as we drove to the emergency room, I realized that she was taking me across the state line into Oklahoma. *Why would she be taking me to Oklahoma to see a doctor?* Tears began to roll down my face as my young mind put the pieces together. *She doesn't want anyone to see me with my face bandaged. She doesn't want them to know what he's done. She is protecting him, again!*

After I got stitched and bandaged up, we got back in the car and headed for home. I was a little confused, though, when we pulled up in front of a house that I didn't recognize.

"Where are we?" I asked my mom, as I looked at this unfamiliar place through the car window.

"Now, this is the home of a very good friend of mine. She and her husband are being very gracious by allowing you to stay here with them until your eye heals up and Dad has a chance to cool down," my mom explained. "You be very good for them and remember, ladies don't talk about their troubles. No one wants to hear a sob story. Just be good and helpful, and you'll be home in no time."

I thought about protesting, but I was actually relieved to be away from my home and the abuse for a while.

This Could Be You

My mom's friend and her husband were an older couple, and I felt like a prisoner in their home. They wouldn't let me go to school, and I wasn't even allowed to go outside because someone might notice my eye and want to know what happened. My older sister and one of my younger brothers were both forced to make up lies about why I was not at school.

This was not the first time I had been pawned off on the neighbors. There were many times when my sister, brothers and I would be dropped off to stay with neighbors while my mom was in the hospital. She was in the hospital frequently due to the physical abuse of my stepdad, although we didn't realize at the time why she was there. My stepdad didn't want to put up with us on his own, so he would make an appeal to the neighbors to help him out while his wife was in the hospital.

If we had had the same neighbors for any amount of time, they might have grown suspicious, but we moved so often that no one ever caught on. Because we moved so often, it was difficult to make friends. I never even finished a whole school year in one place until seventh grade.

Since we didn't have many friends, my sister, brothers and I hated being separated from one another. We felt alone, unwanted and out of place; but it was a relief to be out of our abusive home, if only for a little while.

Even though I couldn't believe my mom would leave me alone after what he had done to me, I at least felt safe in this new place. That feeling didn't last long. One day, while I was staying with these

The Bondage Stops Here

"friends" of my mother's, the woman left to go to the store and her husband came into the bedroom to find me. He kept walking closer and closer to me. "Now, I'm not going to hurt you," he lied, as he put his hands on me. *He's an adult. Do what he says. Don't fight it, and you won't get hurt.* These were the thoughts that kept playing over in my mind as the loathsome man, the one my mother entrusted me to, continued to touch, fondle and degrade me.

I was always too afraid to fight back with adults because of what my stepdad did to us. It was better just to take it than to get hurt worse for resisting. This was in 1970, and nobody talked openly about such things back then. The vile man never acted like anything had happened between us, and I think he was afraid of getting caught because he never touched me again.

There was only one person in my life during this time that seemed to genuinely care about me. My uncle, my mother's youngest brother, was only six years older than me, and from the time I was about 7 years old, my mom would have him babysit me. He was very nice to me, and I finally felt like I had someone who really loved and wanted me around.

My uncle and I had a lot of fun together, and I never had to worry about him hitting me or yelling at me. He took me places like amusement parks and to get ice cream. He even let me hang out in his bedroom and play with his stuff. He really made me feel special.

One day, after we'd been out having fun, we

This Could Be You

came back to his house, which was the home of my grandmother. "Let's go to my room. I've got some cool new things you can play with," he enticed me.

"Yeah!" I cheered as I skipped to his room.

"What is it? What is it?" I wanted to know as I started looking all over his room for something that I hadn't seen before.

"Come over here and sit on my lap, and I'll tell you a secret," he said.

I still thought we were having fun, and I loved being with him, so I went and sat on his lap. He started whispering in my ear, but I couldn't pay attention to what he was saying because I felt his hands touching me in places where no one else had ever touched me before. I knew better than to argue with someone bigger than me, and I didn't want to ruin the one good relationship in my life, so I didn't resist him.

Looking back, I am astonished that my uncle and I were allowed to spend so much unsupervised time together, given our ages. He babysat me often and was allowed to sleep over at our house as much as he wanted. It wasn't until I got older that I realized something wasn't right about our relationship and the things we did when we were alone. Obviously, my home did not set a standard for acceptable behavior.

All of the abuse I suffered at the hands of this boy occurred in either mine or my grandmother's home. Apparently, everyone in my home was oblivious to what was going on. Our relationship continued until my uncle moved away when I was 14.

The Bondage Stops Here

The really ironic thing was that my stepdad forced my siblings and me to go to church. Many times he also made us read from the Bible as a form of punishment.

I remember one time when I was 9 years old. We were at a Sunday morning church service, and I was sitting on the back row of the sanctuary, talking to some of the other kids during the service, not really paying any attention to what the pastor said. All of a sudden, a middle-aged woman with dark hair walked over to me and asked, "Do you love Jesus?"

I didn't really know what she meant, but I didn't want to give her the wrong answer, and it was obvious what she wanted me to say. "Yes," I replied, hoping that she would go away.

"Well, then. You're saved!" she exclaimed. "You need to be baptized," she went on, as she grabbed my hand and dragged me down to the front.

The whole time she was pulling me down the aisle, I was thinking, *Don't you have to make up your own mind to follow Jesus and to be saved?* But it was pretty standard in that church to get saved and baptized at least by the age of 9.

I remember that my stepdad got baptized on that same day. I can still remember what he looked like standing there in the baptismal with his arms crossed. *What a hypocrite!* I thought.

He really had everyone fooled. He went to church and acted all happy and respectful, but as soon as we got home, we could barely get in the door before the abuse started. I wondered if everyone's life was like ours but suspected that they were-

This Could Be You

n't. All the people at church looked so happy and nice, and they seemed to really enjoy their families. What a foreign concept that was to me.

Even though I was "saved and baptized" on that day, it didn't really mean anything to me. It was just one more thing that I was forced to do.

By the time I turned 14, my older sister no longer lived at home. She got pregnant intentionally as an excuse to get out of our house. With her gone, I began looking for excuses to stay away myself. I tried to find any kind of job that would keep me out of my house for as long as possible.

Most days I didn't have any trouble finding a place to go. If I didn't have babysitting jobs, I would hang out at the mall until it closed. Sunday, though, was a different story. Back then, the stores didn't open on Sunday, and pretty much everything was quiet. Everything that is, except for church. Since the church was the only thing open, I would sneak out to the stairwell at the back of the church building and sit on the steps as long as I could.

Eventually, I worked up enough nerve to go inside the building, and I began to listen to the pastor's message. He taught the gospel. He said that salvation was a choice to be made by me, not forced upon me. As I continued to really listen to what he was saying, I knew in my heart that it was time for me to make my own decision. I wanted to be saved. A lady in the church prayed with me, and I turned my heart over to Jesus. Since I had made this choice on my own, I wanted to be baptized again. Neither my mom nor my stepdad came to that service.

The Bondage Stops Here

Finally, when I turned 15, Mom decided she'd had enough abuse of her own and kicked my stepdad out of the house. It was a relief to have him out of our lives.

Even though I accepted Christ as my Savior, I really didn't know what a Christian life was supposed to look like. I had never been around anyone who modeled a life that was ordered by the word of God. So, even though I gave my life to Jesus, it continued to be a very shallow existence for me.

I felt like I had a sign over my head that said, "I'm here for you to abuse me!" I lived a teenage life of sexual promiscuity. I felt like sex was something that was expected of me, and I had no right to say no. I even tried to gain weight so the boys at school would lose interest, but it didn't work. Then a distant relative of my mom's hired me to come clean his house one weekend. The night before I was supposed to clean for him, he came to our house and offered to take me with him then.

"It will save you from having to bring her out tomorrow," he convinced my mom.

And so I went with him. When we got to his house, he began to drink. My plan was to go to bed early, get up early the next day, clean his house and go.

As the night wore on, the man drank more and more. I remember thinking, *He's a lot bigger than me. I'll do whatever he wants, and I won't get hurt. If I try to fight him, there's no telling what will happen, and no one will know because I am way out here.* I had learned a long time before that it was just better not to argue

This Could Be You

with adults. Just do what they want and get it over with.

Eventually, he forced me into the bedroom and raped me. I remember the drunker he got, the stranger he acted. I watched him pee on the floor in the corner of the room. I'm not sure if he thought it was the bathroom, or if he just didn't care.

Finally, he passed out, and I went upstairs to the other end of the house, as far away as I could get, and hid there, trembling, until morning. The next morning, I got up and cleaned the house. After all, that is what I was hired to do. No one else ever knew what happened to me that night. I knew no one would believe me if I told them.

* * *

The memories of all of the abuse I suffered growing up had either been suppressed or denied until the night I saw my husband abusing my son. Then it all came flooding back. I had a mental breakdown, became suicidal and was diagnosed with posttraumatic stress disorder and depression.

I couldn't believe that I had put myself and my children in the same abusive situation that my mother had raised me in. This was my second abusive marriage. *How did I let this happen?* I often questioned.

Even though I hadn't been actively pursuing a relationship with Jesus, it was always very important to me to take my family to church. I believe that I accepted Christ when I was 14, and it was the Holy

The Bondage Stops Here

Spirit that kept drawing me back to him.

Every time I would seek counsel at church, however, I was told, "Don't leave your husband. God hates divorce. Submit to your husband, and pray for him that God will save him."

What am I supposed to do? I remember thinking many times. I was so confused. I wanted to do the right thing, but I didn't know what that was. My mom had been married four times by that point in my life, and I felt like I was following in her footsteps. I felt completely worthless.

Eventually, I became scared enough of my husband that I left him and went to a battered women's shelter. I also had a lot of confusion about God because of what I had been told by people in the church. I never understood why they would let abusive people like my stepdad and my husband hold positions of integrity in the church, or why they would tell me that I had to submit to the abuse.

Fortunately, I started attending a Christian-based support group for abused women. "One of these days," they encouraged me, "you will be able to share your story with other women who are hurting just as bad as you're hurting now, and you'll be able to help them through that hurt." That was in 1993. 14 years later, I think I'm finally ready.

I came to Centralia in 1996 and met John. He was a friendly man who came over to greet me after church one Sunday. I told him, "You don't want to know me. I've got three kids, and I've got baggage. Lots of baggage."

"Well, I've got kids, too, so how about we just all

This Could Be You

hang out together?" he coaxed.

"It doesn't have to be anything serious, just something fun for the kids."

The thought of doing something fun and making new friends was a welcome change, so I agreed, and we started going on outings with his kids and mine. We did casual things together for about a year and eventually became very close friends. I prayed to God during this time to please spare me from any more pain. I didn't want to have anymore failed marriages. If John and I were going to have a relationship, I wanted it to be God's idea and not my own. And if he wanted us to be married, he would have to work out all of the details. Then I would know for sure that it was his will.

We've been married now for eight and a half years, and they have been the happiest, most precious years of my life. Ezekiel 36:11b says, "… I will settle you after your old estates, and will do better unto you than at your beginnings: and ye shall know that I am the Lord." For the first time in my life, I feel settled, and I know my Lord.

John and I started attending Destiny Christian Center in Centralia, and we have a pastor who not only teaches the truth of God's word, but also walks in the truth and encourages others to do the same. He teaches about a God of love and redeeming grace.

I have also attended a ladies' Bible study/support group where we are free to talk about and break free from the bondage of our past.

At our church, I feel loved and accepted. I am not

The Bondage Stops Here

judged because of my past. I am encouraged to let God take the pain of my past and turn it into something beautiful. I know that I am a child of God, I am loved, and I am forgiven.

The most painful regret of my life is that my children suffered a lot of the same types of abuse as I did. If I could have saved anyone from experiencing so much pain, I would definitely want to spare my three children their suffering.

"What kind of loving God could ever let innocent children suffer?" is a question asked often by victims of abuse. I understand why because I asked the same thing. My daughter still struggles with that question, and I see it hindering her ability to break free into a life of redemption.

I believe that from the time we are created, God has a plan for our lives, but there is an enemy who wants more than anything to keep us from achieving it. I have personally experienced the level of depravity and perversion he will inflict upon us to keep us from achieving the plan for which we were created.

Psalms 103:2b-4a says, "… forget not all his benefits: Who forgiveth all thine iniquities; who healeth all thy diseases; who redeemeth thy life from destruction…"

When I lay my past hurts and failures at the feet of Jesus, I received his forgiveness, healing and love. When I refused to forgive, and chose to walk in bitterness and resentment, I gave the enemy power to create strongholds in my life.

I may not be able to go back and recreate the life my children knew, and they may not even want to

This Could Be You

listen to me now, but I know who their true enemy is, and I know that he thrives in the darkness. He took my hurts and frailties and deceived me into believing that if people knew what I'd done, I would be looked down upon. He bombarded my mind with feelings of shame and guilt to the point where I lived in bondage to my past.

Now that I have experienced the freedom of living in God's grace, I will not be shamed into silence about the events of my life and thereby give Satan power over it. I will proclaim who I am in Christ, and I will go to battle every day for my children and others who have suffered the pain of abuse, until I see them experience this same freedom in their own lives.

The Bible says, "Be self-controlled and alert. Your enemy, the devil, prowls around like a roaring lion, looking for someone to devour. Resist him, standing firm in the faith, because you know that your brothers throughout the world are undergoing the same kind of sufferings.

"And the God of all grace, who called you to his eternal glory in Christ, after you have suffered a little while, will himself restore you and make you strong, firm and steadfast. To him be the power forever and ever. Amen." (1 Peter 4:8-11)

I may have inadvertently allowed the devil access to my children through the bondage of my own past and my lack of knowledge about who I was in Christ, but now I know the truth, and the truth has set me free. I will continue to intercede for my children and others and trust that God will do a work in

The Bondage Stops Here

their lives that only he can do.

I think about God and how he watched his only son, Jesus, be physically and verbally abused. How betrayed Jesus must have felt as he was spat on, cursed at and beaten. He even asked, "My God, my God, why have you forsaken me?" (Matthew 27:46b)

Jesus felt the same betrayal by God that I have struggled with. But God didn't leave Jesus, and he didn't leave me. Jesus had to suffer because it meant that we could all be saved. God knew the glory that was waiting for Jesus on the other side of death.

I believe that because I have suffered, many can be healed and restored. I am already experiencing the glory that comes from submitting to God's will, and I am excited about my future and what God has for me.

This may seem like the end of my story, but it's not. It's only the beginning.

Power Source
The Story of John Lund
Written by Richard Drebert

I neglect thoughts of a scorching breach as I work near 2,400 pressurized pounds of searing steam rammed to whirling turbines. Inside a coal-fired power plant, fossil fuel is ground up fine as face powder and ignited in a hellish furnace, where blistering mist is pumped through a maze of tubes. Vibrations in a single bearing or an errant cloud of coal dust outside the boiler can send steam plant technicians scrambling. Lethal methane gas can ignite inside the ductwork (wide as a compact car), where hot air spews at 700 degrees to dry the coal — the explosion can raze a building 50 feet away.

I've been wearing a hardhat in a coal-fired power plant since the 1970s, schooled as a plant equipment operator. I'm one of two dozen troubleshooters who keep the power turbines running at a brisk 3,600 rpm's around the clock. A map of "the big picture" is burned into my brain — how the whole plant functions — and I tread a catwalk of contingencies where more than 60 separate systems run simultaneously, synchronized from a single room of dials, meters and switches. I've learned that a mind riveted on a valve repair, while ignoring all the other systems, can result in tragedy.

And yet, when I was a young man, life's "big picture" seldom fueled my decisions. A sweeping panorama of events shaped me; a power unequaled by

This Could Be You

any human mind worked in my life. I was a middle-aged man before God infused me with a desire to discover my place in the Master's plan, and it took years of failures and victories before I learned how to be a technician in his kingdom.

One Slip

I was well churched as a boy, with a good Lutheran mother and a semi-devout father, and I attended a parochial school where I would have pulled an easy A+ in daydreaming, had it been a subject. Hawthorne, my hometown, was just one of many appendages of Los Angeles; our two-bedroom, single-story house fit snugly in a hive of identical dwellings — 19 to a block — and our neighborhood went on for miles. I lived in the same small house for more than 17 years with my father, mother and older sister.

My mother was a Chicago girl, nicknamed Tootie, and she didn't drive, so she and I often rode the city bus to her favorite stores (the experience still makes me shudder) to ferret through bolts and bolts of fabric. Fastidious to a fault, Mom visited several stores in a day to find that *perfect* color and most reasonably priced material. We always made it home in time for her to spiff up the kitchen, and while I played outside in the flowerbeds with metal pre-Tonka trucks, she created uniquely "Tootie-style" oven-baked spaghetti or mini pizzas. Once a week, we were treated to hearty steaks.

Tootie's husband, Elmer, was an introspective

Power Source

man, a machinist by trade. Dad worked in a factory, making molds for plastic parts, and to me, he seldom seemed like he was home in his mind, unless I needed scolding. As a boy, I learned to discuss my problems with myself; I never told Dad how I felt, and he never asked. As long as I did what was expected, I received my obligatory fathering and the reminder of a good work ethic as a bonus.

Dad had worked in a sheet metal shop out of high school, and while slapping a steel panel in a cutting machine one day, he mistakenly engaged a control while his hand rested beneath a shear. At 18, the accident shredded the blueprint for his future in a trade that required dexterity, and it wasn't until I was grown that he told me how he often hid his misshapen left hand in a pocket to get hired — and sometimes lost the job the same day when the foreman noticed. His trauma set his mind toward depression and alcohol; he left most of the heavy drinking behind when he married Tootie, but the depression haunted him for decades. As a teen, I could never relate to my father's inner turmoil until I faced my own upheavals later, when I learned how a single misstep can change everything.

Dentist Dreams

"I can just *see* John pulling teeth!" Kirsten, my sister, was four years older than me, and making her own way in life while I was finishing high school. "I think he'll faint."

My family loved discussing my future as a den-

This Could Be You

tist, but I felt that I had been left out of the decision. The prospect of sitting through four years of college made me sick inside, but I didn't want to disappoint Mom. I gave Kirsten a practiced glare — one reserved for my only sister — and I glanced at Mom, who smiled as she stitched a rip in a blanket, then at Dad, who sniffed as he folded back a page of the local newspaper.

"He'll do fine," Mom said confidently, and pinched the fabric between her fingers which made her wince a little. Severe arthritis was stealing her satisfaction in needlework and other physical jobs that kept the house running smoothly. There had been talk of moving to a drier, less humid climate to the south, but Dad had balked. At his age, he worried about leaving his solid job in Hawthorne and trying to find work as a handicapped machinist in a new town.

My ambitions idled at a low rpm, guided by my parents who believed my destiny lay with crowns and cavities. In my sophomore year at Trinity Lutheran, I had convinced my parents that I needed to branch out, and I had enrolled at Hawthorne High School, the biggest leap I had ever taken in my sedate young life. In public school, I continued to be "average" and graduated with mediocre grades, my mind barely stretching beyond my hometown of Hawthorne.

One day, my mother sat down with me at the kitchen table, looking serious. "You and I are moving, John. Your father will stay here to work, but our friends in Arizona will help us get settled in a new

Power Source

house there. *And...* there is a wonderful college called the University of Arizona in Tucson where you can prepare for your career as a dentist."

I was excited about moving to a new town, and my parents actually sold the old Hawthorne house. Dad went to live with my grandmother in the Los Angeles area, and Mom and I moved our belongings to Kingman, Arizona. My mother seemed happier and healthier in Kingman; I left her there and headed to my new life as a college kid at a dorm in Tucson. It felt good to be on my own — learning to do my own laundry and balancing my own checkbook. I thrived on my new independence.

My dorm was filled with out-of-state kids just like me, and I made few friendships, since no one was from my hometown. My studying barely produced passing grades the first year, and deep in my heart, I decided that I wasn't cut out for a life of drilling teeth. I was about 20 years old when I thwarted my mother's ambitions for me and quit college. I moved to Kingman and visited the employment office, utterly unprepared for the real world.

Career Castaway

Dishwasher, day laborer, janitor... I tucked the list of uninspiring jobs into a pocket and headed home to our house in Kingman, where Mom was waiting with an ad scissor-snipped from the Kingman newspaper. Bailing out of a dental career had shaken Mom, but she recovered quickly and planned to steer me in a new direction. "John, here, go get this

This Could Be You

job. Southern California Edison is a good company. It is solid, with retirement and benefits."

I felt like a heel for allowing Mom to waste her dreams on me, so I signed up immediately for an aptitude test among applicants spanning the entire Southwestern U.S. A flock of 300 hopefuls showed up at a meeting, and I didn't figure I had a snowball's chance in a furnace to land one of 10 prime jobs at the Mohave Generating Station. I took the tests, and only 25 applicants passed, but I was one of them, and the supervisors chose me and nine others to learn the trade. That's when I *should* have realized that a detailed schematic had been drawn up for my life; God was channeling me into a career where I would thrive, a place to generate his purpose through my life — with a few selfish interruptions along the way.

For the first time in my life, I *loved* school. I was getting paid for learning work that fascinated me at a steam plant in Southern Nevada. The plant sucked its cooling water from the Colorado River, and I lived in Bullhead City near the main complex at Laughlin. After 20 weeks of training, they turned me loose as a plant equipment operator — a troubleshooter for pumps, valves, pipes, generators and turbines — and on call, I responded to a control operator, the overseer of all the systems.

I had been dating Diana on and off since I was in high school, but after my college fiasco, we seriously considered an engagement and married in 1972. For Diana and me, our lives seemed predictable, even settled as I gained seniority at the plant, and she be-

Power Source

gan to think about children. It was the farthest thing from my mind when my world suddenly spun off its axis. The job that fulfilled me evaporated in a cloud of steam, and I would learn a life-altering lesson: My career was not what defined me — it was my *character*.

"John, we're going to have to let you go." My supervisor seemed truly sorry that he had to address the problem at all as he continued. "The company can't keep men who steal equipment."

I stood at my boss' desk with my hardhat in sweaty hands, and the reality of what I had done ignited in my head like a methane explosion. Stupid! I had thrown away my career like a broken bearing. I had fallen in with other plant equipment operators who pilfered from the "rich and wasteful" Southern California Edison, everything from nuts and bolts to slightly used tools rescued from trash bins. At the end of my shifts, I had filched items I needed for home projects during my one and a half years with the company, like everyone else. Somehow, I had justified the theft — until now. Someone had seen me throw a heavy-duty come-along in my pickup truck.

"Look, son. If you quit now, it won't go on your work record *why* we're firing you." I accepted my fate and sheepishly tendered my resignation, worried sick how my family would take it: Diana and especially my mother and father.

At the time, I had no idea that my greatest disappointment as a young man was a tool in God's hands to help me grasp the "big picture" and guide me to

This Could Be You

the truth.

At home, I struggled with regrets while sending out applications to utility companies all over the country, but I got no answers to my queries. Our savings was dwindling, and I was considering a different line of work, when after six long weeks, one reply came from the Northwest.

"Mr. Lund, you are scheduled for an interview at our Pacific Power and Light office..."

I was elated and pulled out a map of Washington State to find Centralia, where the coal-fired power plant was located. I had one more chance to salvage my vocation — if I could impress the hiring agent and get past the six-month probation period.

"I've got to go to the PP&L office in Centralia for an interview," I told Diana, and we started packing.

I got my interview. I got my medical tests in Portland where a woman gave me a specific time to call back, and on the way home to Arizona, I pulled over to make the critical call. I expected bad news; I felt that the interview in Centralia hadn't been a shining success.

"So, when would you like to start work?"

I hung up the phone in shock.

"I got it. I got the job! I start on Monday."

I drove through the main gate of the Centralia Steam Plant and felt electrified. My new workplace stretched for miles and included a surface coalmining operation, a river dam for its water supply and a roaring generation complex from which electricity surged to the Northwestern U.S. and Canada. I remembered the location of the main office and jogged

Power Source

up the steps to resuscitate my career.

"And *why* do you think that you have a job here at PP&L?"

Inside my chest, I felt like a main valve had shut off the blood supply. "I... I was hired from the Portland office." I handed my paperwork to the glowering supervisor.

"Well, we haven't heard anything about it." He spoke like his home turf had been violated, and a deathly silence invaded the fluorescent-lit room while he fumbled for his glasses. He read my hiring documents, and I revived a little when he mumbled and pointed to the waiting room. "Hmm, I'll be with you in a minute." The door closed.

A phone call was made. There was murmuring, and then my new boss emerged. "Mr. Lund, you're hired, with a six-month probation period." I noticed an amused gleam in his eyes after I over-zealously pumped his arm. It felt good to breathe again, and I trotted off for my orientation — *and just the edge of God's "big picture" unfurled a little in my heart.* Someone was interested in me. Someone was revealing my purpose for living, though I barely comprehended the loving source who worked on my behalf.

Finding My Source

I lost myself in learning everything I could about the Centralia Steam Plant, and I excelled in my work, rotating in and out of five different jobs in different areas of the plant. At home, my wife and I prepared for a new addition to our family. When my daughter

This Could Be You

was born, her innocence opened a fresh burst of wonderment in my soul. Eternity somehow reflected in her eyes, and I began to hunger to know more about God and his plans.

In a coal-fired plant, every watt of power can be traced to its source — not one system works alone — and I began pondering the source that had an obvious hand in my own life. Church seemed the best place to find answers, and Diana wanted to go, too, so we found a very reserved Lutheran church to attend, as we built our family with two other children.

If you are a droplet of water inside the "closed system" of a steam plant, your journey begins inside a condenser and you flow through a tube to a heated boiler where you turn to steam. Mingling with other expanding steam molecules, you power turbines that run generators that produce electricity. After the job is done, steam cools and flows right back to the condenser to become a droplet of water, and the process begins again.

For several years, I lived in my own "closed system." I was working at the Centralia plant, attending to my family's needs, going to church for moral tuning and doing it all over again. But I lived with a nagging thought that I missed something *important*, like I had forgotten to check a critical gauge or to grease up a bearing.

Studying the Bible with other men at church filled some of my yearning, and the group leader had asked our pastor *not* to attend, so that we could open up without feeling like we were under church scrutiny — and indeed we did.

Power Source

"Man, something is happening with my wife," a young man told us one evening. "She says she 'got the Holy Spirit,' and, you know, she just isn't the same woman!" He went on to describe how joyful she was, and something in the depths of my soul *leaped*. I needed to know more. I began to study scriptures in the New Testament that I had skipped over and realized that this Holy Spirit *filling* was part of the experience of the first Christians.

For the first time, I applied the words in the Bible directly to me: God's power, beyond natural understanding, was available to anyone who accepted Christ and asked for the filling of his Holy Spirit. I had accepted Christ — was there anything that prevented me from asking for his "filling?" It was right there in the Bible. Why had no one taught me this exciting truth that miracles followed those who believed?

Working with boiling water and searing steam, coal gases and fire, I live by one prevailing principle: *Safety first*. Reams of paperwork cross the desks of supervisors regarding new safety plans, and no one is more tuned to safe work conditions than I. But in my life as a Christian, I made a decision to leave what I believed to be the "safety" of the Lutheran doctrine and seek the face of my God in the simplicity of his word. And I wasn't the only one. A small group of "charismatic" Lutherans had begun to worship together at our church. I *felt* the presence of God at these gatherings, and I began to ask Jesus to fill me with his Holy Spirit — just like he did for his disciples in the book of Acts.

This Could Be You

Lutherans are taught to stay in the fold; straying into other churches is frowned upon. So when a friend invited me to attend Living Waters, a Pentecostal church, I resisted a feeling of condemnation when I decided to attend. The freedom among the people there astonished me, and those I spoke to understood exactly what I was looking for.

"Oh, I received the Holy Spirit a year ago — and my life has been so different!"

"I've seen so many miracles in my family since I received the Holy Spirit." To these folks, the experience was as familiar and important as communion, and their testimonies ramped up my hopes. I drove my car home after the service, and the yearning in my heart amplified like the powering up of a generator — *I needed to go back*. I hadn't received what I came for.

The pastor seemed to be waiting for me, and I barely held my emotions in tact as I told him my heart's desire to receive the empowering of the Holy Spirit. It was that simple: Prayer. Praise with upraised hands. Jesus filled me. For the next few nights, I lay in bed, worshiping God in ways I had never experienced, and at last, God engraved his "big picture" upon my heart. Understanding that Jesus had a specific *purpose* for me changed my view of life, and suddenly, other men I had worked with for years connected with me because they were Christians, too. My joy was contagious.

In the following weeks, I generated controversy with the leadership of our church as I "lived out" my faith, and in time, I left the Lutheran faith to fellow-

Power Source

ship with brothers and sisters who perceived the "big picture" of the Bible in the fullest measure, without snipping out the verses that defy human explanation. But I set my new course without empathy, and like my first days at the steam plant, I experienced a learning curve as I judged the motives of others. It took time for God to teach me gentleness and humility as I learned about my spiritual gifts, and Jesus was gracious to use me, imperfect as I was. It took time to discern the voice of Christ amid all of life's noise when he was "nudging" me to pray for someone in need.

Healing Virtue

The singing was particularly sweet at our church the day I felt the Holy Spirit "nudge" me to pray for Julie, an older woman who suffered from a kidney disease. Doctors had refused to operate a third time to remove blockages, and she had been living in extreme pain. As I turned to her in the pew behind me, I laid my hands on her tummy and prayed for Jesus to heal her. Immediately, in my mind, I saw a picture of tubes knotted and bent at sharp angles in all directions.

"Oh, *Jesus*," she said, and under my hands, it felt like water roiled inside her. In my mind, the scene suddenly changed, and I watched the tubes unknot and unbend. A few days later, Julie testified about her experience.

"As Brother Lund prayed for me, I felt a burning inside." Julie related how she knew she had been

This Could Be You

healed when the pain — so common during her everyday physical functions — had vanished.

And God has confirmed his healing power *and mercy* in my own life, too.

***

Pain throbbed inside my eye, and tears overflowed uncontrollably. I was on my knees praying, my heart sinking in defeat and loss as I remembered how I had skirted God's warning: *Don't cut up firewood today.* I had "parsed" the message when my son asked me to cut up a downed tree that lay across his fort — I wasn't really "cutting firewood." Now, I realized my mistake.

A springy hazelnut branch whipped from beneath the log I had chattered through with my chainsaw, striking me full in the left eye. I shut down the saw, and after a few moments, stumbled to the house, praying aloud for God to forgive me for disregarding his voice and asking for his healing virtue to flow to my eye. When I finally opened my eye, the world appeared opaque, like I squinted through a cloud, and at once, I sensed his words strongly: *I will restore your eye.* I knew the promise was for me.

An hour later, the eye doctor seemed shocked at the amount of damage one branch had inflicted. "I haven't seen a lens torn this bad," he said, but diagnosed that it would mend. He wanted to see me again the next day. "In the meantime, you better be ready to use up your sick days," he said.

Power Source

I didn't want to be rude, but the Holy Spirit was speaking so loudly in my heart that I barely heard what the doctor was saying, and I wasn't about to shut out God's words: *I will restore your eye.* At home, I rested and continued to believe what God had spoken. The following day, the doctor shined a light into my eyeball, and he seemed baffled.

"John, your eye is perfectly healed." He shined the light again and shook his head. "I wouldn't have believed that you had an accident yesterday, if I hadn't been the doctor who examined you. I think your sight should return to normal in a few days, too."

He was wrong about the time it would take for the "murkiness" to vanish. Two months later, I still struggled with cloudiness and depth perception, and at work, I chose jobs that usually didn't require two good eyes, until God spoke to me once again: *You need to act like you are healed.*

Welding is a job that takes two good eyes, as well as skill, and I decided to grab onto God's promise with both hands when I was assigned a project at the plant one day. I flipped down my helmet, prayed a quick thanks and fired up the welder. As I laid down a bead, I noticed improvement in my vision, including depth perception. After running a few more beads, I started shouting into my helmet, praising God for healing me. My heart overflowed, and when I looked at my hand, I marveled! God had restored clear vision to my injured left eye.

But as I paused to gaze for a few moments at the mountains in the distance, the sight in my eye faded to a milky tone once again. I fought down a sense of

This Could Be You

fear and immediately remembered the admonition in the Bible: *Walk by faith, not by sight.* I flipped my welding helmet over my face again and lit up the arch in faith. From that day forward, my eye has been completely restored.

Our Destiny

Some might think that a man or woman to whom the Holy Spirit imparts his gifts must be immune to fleshly weaknesses and trials, but I assure you, *everyone* operating in the gifts of the Spirit is vulnerable to lapses in judgment, or can choose to deliberately sin. God is not picky when it comes to doling out his gifts to those yearning for a spiritual awakening; God's objective is to confirm his word with real-world miracles and draw people to a decision for Jesus.

In my case, even while operating in a healing ministry, my marriage relationship began to erode. I could not save my union, and the guilt and pain over my divorce stole away the joy of serving Jesus for a time. My heart was broken, and I sought God's emotional healing, falling back into that "closed system" that held me captive for so many years.

But the Holy Spirit hadn't forgotten the man he had lovingly filled to overflowing. Words fail me in describing how intimately Jesus has ministered to me! He has healed my emotional wounds and introduced me to a committed helpmate who ministers with her own gifts from the Holy Spirit; now, our blessings overflow in a church dedicated to drawing

Power Source

hurting people to Jesus. For the last several years, I have taught Sunday school classes, Bible studies and home groups at Destiny Christian Center, and I serve with others who see people healed of their emotional and physical pain — just like Jesus did for me!

Together, this has become *our* Destiny.

A Letter to Jennifer
The Story of Gary
Written by Angela Prusia

"Dear Dad," the letter read. "It was nice to visit with you this weekend. Seeing you with your granddaughter makes me smile. I know she's got you wrapped around her finger, even though she's only a baby, but I can see a great change in you.

"I can't really describe the difference in you exactly. Where I saw pain before, I now see joy. It's like all the shame and suffering you carried around for so long is wiped away. You're just not the same, Dad. You didn't cuss once during the entire visit, and your attitude was way better.

"I know you loved me before, but your love seems stronger somehow. When you want to pray for me whenever we talk on the phone now, I get choked up. I love you, Dad. Love, Jennifer."

I wiped away the tears. Who would've thought a messed-up drug addict could be reduced to mush? If I could bottle up the years I suffered because of my addictions, one whiff and the stench would kill me. I look back and see the man chained by sin. Each link cemented my desperation. I was hopeless, lost and desperate.

I'd told my daughter bits and pieces of my life, but maybe it was time for the whole story. Jennifer, this is my letter to you.

This Could Be You

***

I sat on top of the sand dune and fingered the two marijuana joints in my pocket. My friends and I loved to build forts in the mangrove island when we were kids. It wasn't far from my home in the Keys, and the grassy dunes created the perfect cover.

My parents were busy entertaining relatives from Michigan, so I wouldn't be missed for a couple hours. If I was lucky, they'd be sloshed by the time I got home.

I put the joint to my mouth like I'd seen my friend do when we were hanging out, listening to music.

"What're you smoking?" I'd asked.

"Pot." He sold me two joints for a dollar.

I sucked on the stick like a cigarette. I'd been smoking for a while.

I wished I wasn't alone now.

"What's the big deal?" I murmured when I finished the joint. I crushed it in the sand with my foot. "I feel the same."

The second joint freaked me out. I could see one of my older friends at the gas station a block away.

"Dude, you reek," he said when I approached him. "Are you high?"

I was scared. "Will I be like this forever?" I felt like I could explode with energy.

He laughed. "Run around the gas station four or five times, and you'll feel better."

I started to sprint.

"Dude, I'm teasing. Hang out here. You'll be

A Letter to Jennifer

okay." He laughed. "And get some gum. It'll help the smell."

I felt my pocket for loose change and saw several coins fall onto the ground. They flipped over and bounced back up to me.

"Weird." I watched in fascination. The rational part of me knew I was tripping out.

I popped a gumball into my mouth. Gum had never tasted so good. My taste buds were on overdrive, heightening the flavor.

My sense of time was off, too. I figured I better get home before I got in trouble.

"What are you doing?" my dad asked me when I tried to escape the relatives.

"Going to bed." It wasn't as late as I'd thought — only 8:30 — but I couldn't hang out with the family. I was still high.

I lay on my bed and turned to the wall when my brother came into the room.

"What're you doing in bed?" He was 10 years older than me.

"I'm tired," I lied.

"Look at me. You smell like weed."

I turned to face him.

"You're stoned. I can see it in your eyes."

I asked him if he was going to tell.

My brother shook his head. "If you touch the stuff again, I'll beat your butt." A week later, my brother had a favor to ask. "Can you get me some of that pot?"

My eyes bugged out. "But…"

"Forget what I said," he laughed. "I was just

This Could Be You

messing with you."

That's all it took. I was hooked on drugs as a sixth grader.

***

"You little thief!" My dad lunged for me. I tried to escape, but he was stronger than me. He was tough, a master sergeant in the military.

"I didn't take your money," I lied.

"Don't give me that bull," my dad yelled. "My wallet's gone."

Curses flew as my dad beat me.

"Stop," I protested, but my dad was furious. I shielded my face with my arms.

"Don't let me ever catch you stealing from me again."

"I won't," I promised as the pounding subsided. But my addiction was more powerful than my word. I had to get sneakier. I couldn't live without my fix. I was too young to see the chains that clamped an iron grip around me.

***

I cast the line into the water and wedged my pole into some rocks, so I could roll a joint.

"I wanna smoke, too." Chris eyed me as he reeled in his line.

"What if your geeky brother finds out?"

"He won't," Chris smiled. "He's too busy being good."

A Letter to Jennifer

"You were good until I corrupted you."

Chris laughed as he pulled out his money. "How much?"

Before long, he was buying from me on a regular basis. By high school, I couldn't think of one kid on our upscale block that wasn't getting high.

***

My parents suspected my drug use, but they were too addicted to alcohol to see my problems. They accepted that I smoked and encouraged me to drink. Sometimes, I would push the limit just to see if they'd say no, but they never did.

"You wanna go with me?" my father asked me one night after my mom was asleep. We stopped at the store for a case of beer and headed to my brother's trailer.

"Have a brewsky." My dad handed me a beer. I was 13.

I'd finished off my dad's cans before, but I'd never had much alcohol. Three beers later, I was jumping on the bed. I laughed along with my father and brother. I was one of the guys.

When my dad and I got home, my mother was awake. She took one look at me and tore into my dad. "You got him drunk."

I gripped my stomach. I didn't feel so good.

"Look at him!" my mother yelled.

My dad smiled. "I guess he drank more than I thought."

"It's not funny," my mom snapped, as she helped

This Could Be You

me to my room. My dad just smirked.

***

I got stuck watching my niece and nephew again because my parents were drinking, and I was mad. I resented the fact that I always had to drag them with me everywhere I went. My mom refused to have anything to do with my brother after he abandoned Tammy and Jay, but we still had to raise them until my sister took them to Iowa. They were watching cartoons with me in my room when my dad knocked on the door.

"You need to come with me, Gary," he said.

I followed him into the master bedroom.

"I think your mom's dead."

I stared at the body crumpled on the floor and felt the panic overtake me. "Do something!" I screamed. I took my mother in my arms and tried mouth-to-mouth resuscitation.

"It's no use." My father's expression was blank. He raised his hand like a zombie and pointed to the bucket beside the bed. Pills floated in the vomit from her overdose. Helplessness washed over me. I was 14. I still needed my mother.

I tried to talk to my friends about my mother's suicide, but they were as messed up as me. Later, a counselor asked me to write a letter to my mother, but I don't remember much about what I wrote. How could I explain the emptiness her death left? People thought I was so tough because I got in a lot of fights, but did they see the boy who cried himself

A Letter to Jennifer

to sleep at night? I got in trouble at school all the time because I couldn't stand the pain that ate me up inside. Drugs were something I always figured I could quit, but now they helped me escape the nightmare that was my life.

***

"You're high again." My stepmom confronted me when I got home from skiing with my friends.

I grunted. I hated her for thinking she could take the place of my mother.

"I'm telling your father," she said.

Something inside me snapped. I whipped out my diver's knife and threatened her. "Leave me alone, or I'll use this." I meant what I said. I'd stab her in the face.

She backed down, but when my dad got home, I got a major beating. I hated the woman.

***

"You wanna talk to your brother?"

I looked at my dad in surprise. "You got his number?" I hadn't talked to my brother since Mom told him the family wouldn't have anything to do with him. Now that she was gone, maybe I'd get to see him more.

"He called the other day," my dad said. "Give him a call."

I reached for the phone, and the two of us talked several times over the next few days.

This Could Be You

"What do you think about moving up to Spokane with your brother?" my dad asked. "Washington's great. You could hunt and fish. You'd love it up there."

Anything sounded better than life with my stepmom. I moved in with my brother and enrolled in a work program through school. I liked working at the civic theater, but when the program wasn't refunded, I dropped out of school altogether.

One Saturday, my brother came home half drunk from a tennis match.

"What are you doing?" I asked. He sat on his bed holding a gun.

"Playing Russian Roulette." My brother spun the cylinder, and the whir was magnified in the silence. He pointed the gun to his head and pulled the trigger. "Bang."

Nothing happened.

"You don't have a bullet in there," I argued. I couldn't believe the gun was loaded.

"You wanna play?"

I grabbed the gun and fired a blank. "This is stupid."

I turned to walk out of the room, and the gun went off. A sharp pain pierced my flesh.

"You got me." I crumpled to the floor in shock.

"No!" my brother screamed. Tears filled his eyes. "Hang on, little brother. Don't you die on me." He was wailing as he picked me up and raced to the hospital.

Later, my doctor told me he'd never seen a bullet wound like mine — even with his service in Viet-

A Letter to Jennifer

nam. "You should be crippled for life, Gary." He pointed to my x-ray. "But it's like something guided the bullet around your spine." The doctor shook his head in disbelief. "You're one lucky kid." I know better now.

***

Even though I was partying all the time, loneliness tore me up inside. My body was so used to the drugs, it took more to get me high. I hated my dependency, and the remorse was like acid poured on my conscience. Life became a two-edged sword. I couldn't live without the drugs, and yet I despised my addictions.

I met some friends from a Baptist church, and one of them took me in when I moved out of my brother's place.

"I just have three rules," Darrol told me when I plopped down on his couch.

"Shoot," I said.

"No smoking in the apartment, no drinking, and you gotta go to church on Sundays."

"No problem," I answered in a coherent moment. I broke the rules the first week.

Darrol showed me God's love even though I didn't know it. I'd never met someone so patient.

"Are you okay?" he asked me when I came home with a hangover.

I just wanted to sleep, but the guy fixed me breakfast. I couldn't understand him.

"What's up with you?" I asked Darrol. Deep

This Could Be You

down, I wanted the peace I saw in his eyes.

"What do you mean?"

"You don't smoke, you don't drink, and you don't mess around with women. It's like you're not normal."

Darrol laughed, but his gaze was intense. "I'm a Christian, Gary."

"I believe in God, too, but I don't live like you do." I had tons of questions, and Darrol answered them all.

I accepted Jesus, but I wasn't ready to change my lifestyle. Ironically, I didn't want to give up the "control" drugs gave me. I felt powerless without them. I couldn't face the inner me. I was terrified people would see the weak Gary — the insecure guy behind the mask.

I went to church and found kids that would drink and do drugs with me. At first, I thought hanging out with my new friends was cool, but then the familiar hopelessness set in. I wanted the peace I saw in Darrol. I wanted to be free of the angry grip of my addictions.

"You need help, Gary," Darrol told me one day.

I shrugged.

"I'm gonna ask Pastor what we can do."

A few weeks later, I made a one-year commitment to New Life Foundation. Three pastors and a friend drove me to Brady. Most of the drug treatment places were full in Spokane, so they wanted to check out the place for others like me.

Withdrawal was miserable. For the first 90 days, I had no access to alcohol or drugs. The fog lifted, and

A Letter to Jennifer

my head began to clear. After six months, participants were encouraged to move back to society. I got a job at a gas station in Olympia and met a girl. I left the program and moved in with her. I desired to change, but I didn't. Drugs made me forget my feelings of failure.

"I'll pray for you," Darrol said when I told him I left the program. I knew he meant it, but the pull of drugs was too strong. I was still young, the voices whispered. Life's one big party.

***

Life became an endless cycle of drugs, booze and women. I couldn't keep a job, but I managed to find women who'd support me. I was tall, so I'd been getting into bars even before I turned 21. I got in a lot of fights, so I spent some time in jail. Life was miserable unless I could get stoned. That was the only way I could tolerate myself.

I got married, but that didn't change anything. I cheated on my wife just like I'd done with every relationship I'd ever had. What remorse I felt was heaped on top of every other thing I'd done to disappoint people.

"We gotta talk," my wife said one day.

Here it comes, I thought. *We're through. She found out I'd cheated on her.*

"I'm having a baby."

My mouth dropped open. "What am I gonna do?"

My wife cursed. "What are you gonna do? I'm

This Could Be You

the one with the kid. What am I gonna do?"

Reality hit me in shock waves. I was going to be a father. I was 25. It was time to grow up, but I couldn't get away from my addictions. The nine months were a blur of drugs, alcohol and women. In rare coherent moments, I knew I'd be the worst father in the world.

"I'm having contractions," my wife said when I came home at two in the morning.

"I'm drunk. I can't go to the hospital." I hit the bed. "Let me sleep awhile."

Hands shook me. "Wake up, Gary."

"Take a taxi. Let me sleep some more," I grunted.

"You don't understand," my wife roared. "I'm having our baby."

I stumbled outside and returned within minutes. "Where's the car?"

My wife gripped her stomach. "I hid it from you. It's over a couple blocks."

My head throbbed as I wandered around the block. *Was it right or left that she said?* When I came home a second time, my wife wasn't happy.

"Get me some paper!" she screamed as another contraction hit. She drew me a map, and this time, I came back with the car. We arrived at the hospital at 5:55 a.m.

"I'm having a baby." My wife gripped the nurse.

"Every first time mom feels this way," the nurse said sweetly. She tried to pry off my wife's fingers. "You're hurting me, honey."

"You haven't seen anything yet!" my wife barked. She silenced me with her look. "And you're

A Letter to Jennifer

next."

Our daughter, Jennifer, was born at 6:07 a.m.

***

Looking into my little girl's face, I resolved to change. I was disgusted with myself. I went to work more often and tried to get my life back. The harder I tried, the worse life got. I went to Alcoholics Anonymous after I got a DWI, but when I slipped, I sunk further into my addiction. I was miserable. Hopeless. Empty. Dead.

"Help me, or leave me alone," I cursed God one night. "I've tried everything and failed. What more can I do?"

The next day, I was surprised to wake up without a hangover.

I went for a pop and ran into one of my friends from rehab. "Unholy alliance," is what the counselors called me and Jiggs. We were always pulling some kind of stunt.

He was surprised I had a wife and kid; I was surprised when he asked me to go to church. We started to hang out, and again, I thought things were looking up. But soon we shared a few beers, and before long, we were robbing places.

My wife tried to enroll me in an inpatient treatment program, but I only lasted three weeks. She wanted a divorce, so I moved in with another woman. I'd already failed my daughter, and she wasn't even old enough to talk. What would she call me? Loser, reject, worthless? Words couldn't express

This Could Be You

the pitiful person I'd become.

***

Just when the vicious cycle couldn't get worse, the alcohol and drugs wouldn't satisfy, so I turned to pornography. I had my favorite porn shops that I would visit. The owners would let me stay after hours in exchange for drugs.

I broke up with my new girlfriend and moved in with another woman. I started working at a foundry, a job I kept for five years — a record for me. One of my coworkers gave me a truckload of porn that I loaded into my Corvette. I thought I'd won the lottery.

I wasn't surprised when my newest relationship failed, too. We'd talked about marriage, but then she found out I'd cheated on her. I should've been upset, but I wasn't. I didn't blame any of the women that left me. I'd leave me, too, if only I could. My heart was so hard, little affected me anymore.

***

"You know I'm the reason you're a heathen," my brother said one day.

I gave a bitter laugh.

"I'm serious," he said, and I knew he was. He'd gotten his life together. "Bonnie and I are praying for you."

"Don't bother," I grunted. He and his wife were always talking to me about the Bible since they re-

A Letter to Jennifer

dedicated their lives to God. He was tired of being phony. "Once you really experience God," he said, "there's nowhere else to go."

I didn't want to hear it; I felt too convicted.

"Things can be better," my brother said.

"Whatever."

"There is hope," he said, but I didn't believe him. How could someone like me ever change? I was hopeless. There was nothing I hadn't tried. And nothing that worked. I couldn't get rid of my addictions. I understood why my mother had ended her life. *What was there to live for?* Maybe I should just end it all.

"I like my life just fine," I lied.

"I'm still gonna pray for you."

I shrugged. Even a miracle couldn't help me.

And yet, a miracle is exactly what happened.

I was sitting on my couch one day, feeling sorry for myself, when I saw my Bible. Something stirred within me, and before I knew it, I was weeping. Emotions I had locked away erupted. I sobbed like I'd never cried before.

"Help me!" I begged. "Lord, if you're there, help me."

I was sobbing so hard, my body shook. I knew I was a sinner. Every mistake I'd ever made stretched to the sky, mocking me.

"You fool," my past cried. "Who could forgive someone like you?"

I prayed so hard, crocodile tears fell from my eyes.

Without warning, a presence flooded over me in

This Could Be You

a tidal wave. Suddenly, everything I'd learned about Jesus dying on the cross for me became clear. I wasn't hopeless. I couldn't change on my own, but Jesus could change me. His gift was for me.

I jumped up and called my brother. He was as dumbfounded as me.

***

Life hasn't been the same since. At age 48, I have hope for the first time in my life. Peace has flooded my soul. I feel free, cleansed of the addictions that robbed so much. I feel happy, confident and blessed. I've been touched by my Maker, and I'll never be the same.

I bought my first house because I wanted to live somewhere more permanently. I even want to go to work as a custodian at the college. I can't wait to go to church, and I'm excited to see my family at Destiny Christian Center.

God has changed my wife, too. She was into astrology and divination when I told her I had changed. If we were going to be together, she would need to meet Jesus, too. Praise God, she did. Sometimes, I feel like we're on our honeymoon because our relationship is so different.

My wife introduced me to Destiny Christian Center. Now she's the one who is ruthless in her Bible study, even keeping me on track. When she was asked to direct the "Clothes and Loaves" program run by our church, I don't know who was happier — me or her. It's this authentic love in action that spurs

A Letter to Jennifer

me to want to know Christ more.

Do I still stumble? Yes, but the desire is gone. Something actually snapped inside me when I renounced the porn and threw the junk in the trash.

I've been clean from drugs for a few years, and I'm learning to pray when I feel powerless over the alcohol. The more I pray, the more God takes over. His intervention is the only power that changes.

***

Jennifer:

Do you remember when you tripped on the curb and scraped your knee real bad? You didn't get stitches, but you still have that scar.

I have a scar that runs across my heart. The wound has been sliced open so often, the scar tissue formed a solid knot. Over time, my heart grew so hard, nothing could penetrate that wound. I know I wasted so many years of our lives together. Sorry seems so little when I regret so much.

I've met a physician who knows how to heal the wounds not seen by man. Slowly, he's stripping away every layer, exposing the hardness. Forgive me for ever hurting you.

I know you saw your mother leave this world in peace despite the tumor that ravaged her brain. And I know you've heard of the physician who's been working on me.

Looking at you is like looking in a mirror with my reflection staring back. I pray that you will really get to know the physician, and he will heal you, too,

This Could Be You

especially in the places I've wounded you. I'm so sorry.

You're always in my heart, Jennifer. I'm so proud of you. I see how hard you work at college, and I know you'll succeed in working with drug and alcohol addicts. There is hope.

I love you, Jennifer.

Love, Dad

Steadfast Love
The Story of Kristi
Written by Amanda Lawrence

I stared down at the plus sign on the test, amazed. I dropped down on the closed toilet lid, and the test hung limply from my fingertips. After four months of trying, I was finally pregnant. My stomach flipped with excitement, and a grin crept across my face. *I'm pregnant. I'm pregnant!* I wanted to shout it, jump up and down and spin in circles. Instead, I opened the bathroom door and calmly called to my husband in the bedroom. "Shad, could you please come here?"

I stood, holding the pregnancy test behind my back. "What is it?" he asked, coming into the room half-dressed.

"I have some news for you." I paused for a moment. "I'm pregnant!"

"Really?" he grinned, then grabbed me around the waist, picked me up and hugged me. "We're going to have a baby?"

"We're having a baby," I exclaimed, grinning back at him. I kissed him, thrilled that I had a little one growing inside of me. He lowered me to the floor, his arms still around my waist.

"Soon, I won't be able to fit my arms around you," he declared. "And I can't wait. I'm so happy."

"Me, too," I agreed. "But we'd better hurry, or we'll both be late." He left the bathroom, and I turned around to turn on the shower. After adjusting

This Could Be You

the hot and cold taps, I undressed. Looking in the mirror at my still flat stomach, I rubbed my hand across my abdomen. *I'm so happy you're in there, little one. I'll take good care of you. I'm going to love watching you grow and feel you inside me. I love you already,* I thought. The mirror started to fog up, so I stepped into the shower and let the warm water rush over my head.

Over the next eight weeks, I experienced a little morning sickness but had no complications. I went to my family doctor for a checkup.

"I'd like to do an ultrasound on you," he told me.

"That'd be great. Shad's in the waiting room," I responded. The doctor called the nurse in to set up the equipment, and he went to get Shad. He stood at my shoulder, holding my hand as the doctor exposed my belly, applied the cold gel-like goop and then proceeded to move the sonogram probe across my stomach.

He stared at the monitor. "Your uterus looks a little enlarged," he commented.

"I know that I have an enlarged uterus," I told him.

He nodded and continued to move the probe. "Everything looks good to me. See the head? And here is the heart pounding," he pointed out on the screen. I looked up from my position on the table and followed his finger as he showed me my baby. I smiled up at Shad, relieved that everything was okay. He squeezed my hand, and the doctor pulled the probe away and turned off the machine. Wiping off my belly, he pulled my top back down. "You and

Steadfast Love

the baby are in good health," he reassured me.

"Thank you, Dr. Watkins," I replied.

"Are you planning on going to an obstetrician before too long? You are at 12 weeks," he asked.

"Yes, I plan on going to one for the remainder of my pregnancy," I told him. "Thank you for all you've done."

"You're welcome, and if you need anything in the meantime, please call," he remarked before going out the door.

Being pregnant was thrilling. The only downfall was Shad having to be out of town so much for work. He couldn't experience all the changes my body was going through. I watched daily as my stomach grew a little more. What had started out as a little thickening blossomed into a round, protruding stomach. Whenever Shad was in town, he loved placing his arms around me to see how much the baby had grown. "Growing by leaps and bounds. One of these days, I won't be able to wrap my arms around the two of you," he would tease.

I went to the obstetrician for my triple screen test in mid-November. Shad was out of town yet again. On Friday of that same week, I came home to find a message on the answering machine. "This is Maryanne at Dr. Taylor's office. We got back your triple screen results and have some concerns with one of the tests that we would like to clear up. We'd like you to come in Monday morning for an ultrasound. Please call our office to set up a time." Beep.

Concerns? What could be wrong? Is something wrong with my baby? I don't even know its sex yet, and some-

This Could Be You

thing shows up on the test. Oh, why isn't Shad here? I'd better call him so he can get home this weekend, so he'll be here to go with me to the ultrasound. I'm not going alone. What if there is something really wrong? I've heard that sometimes there's a fluke with these tests. Something shows up abnormal and everything is okay. Maybe that will be my case. Nothing is wrong. Oh, but what if this isn't a fluke? What if something is really wrong? I thought. *No! Nothing is wrong. Everything is okay.* "Satan, you are not welcome in my thoughts. Get away," I demanded out loud, realizing that all my worries would do no good, and that Satan was feeding my fear. *Lord, please be with me this weekend as I wait. Take my worries away. I believe that everything is okay with my baby,* I prayed and instantly felt peace.

I called Shad. "Honey, can you get home by Sunday night?" I asked after he answered his cell phone.

"Is something wrong?" he asked.

"Dr. Taylor's office called and found something in one of my tests that concerned them. They want me in on Monday morning for an ultrasound. I'd like it if you could be there," I answered.

"I'll be home Sunday night. I promise," he responded. He was.

On Monday morning, we went to Dr. Taylor's office for the ultrasound. The machine hummed after she turned it on, and the jelly wasn't as cold this time. "You've had an ultrasound before?" she questioned.

"Yes, at 12 weeks," I told her, watching the screen as she moved the probe around my distended belly. She was quiet for a moment as she searched the

Steadfast Love

screen. Dark spots and lines showed up here and there as she moved the probe quickly over my stomach.

"So you know that it's twins then?" she asked, still looking at the screen.

"Twins?" Shad and I exclaimed simultaneously.

"No, we didn't know it was twins," I concluded, stunned.

"Well, it's twins," she smiled. "See. Here's Baby A and here's Baby B," she pointed out on the screen. She moved the probe around some more, continuing to point out the heartbeats, legs, arms and heads of each of the babies. "And they look healthy. Everything looks fine." She turned from the monitor and saw our shocked faces, mouths still gaping. "A little hard to take in, especially at 20 weeks?" she asked.

"It's surprising. I realize I'm big, but didn't even think of twins. I didn't feel two of them moving around in here," I replied, patting my stomach.

"Well, congratulations," she declared.

"Thank you," we both murmured.

I looked at Shad. "Twins," I whispered.

"Twins," he whispered back. We grinned.

***

I grew up in Vancouver, Washington, the oldest of three, my sister two years younger and my brother four years younger. My dad worked as a police officer for the Sheriff's office, and while we were young, my mom stayed home with us. As we got older, she worked as the school bus driver and in the

This Could Be You

school cafeteria. We were a close-knit, extended family, spending a lot of time with my nine cousins on my dad's side. We would have picnics and parties just to get together and have fun.

When I was 4 years old, we gathered at the park for a barbecue picnic for my Uncle Marvin, who was leaving for the Navy. Grandpa was always on the playground with us kids, not socializing with the adults.

"Come down and I'll catch you," Grandpa called up to me, standing at the bottom of the slide. My shorts-clad bottom hit the wood at the top of the slide, and I grinned down at him, anticipating the belly flop sensation of whizzing down the metal. I pushed off and soared down.

"Whee," I exclaimed, giggling when I reached the bottom and right into his arms. He swung me up and around to his back, patting my bottom from behind and then holding it. "Grandpa, please let me down," I expressed.

"Not yet. Let me carry you around a little longer," he replied.

"Please, Grandpa, I want down," I pleaded, feeling uncomfortable with his hand on my bottom. "Please let me down," I cried.

"Don't you want me to carry you back to the slide?" he asked with his hand still in place.

"No, I want to walk. Cindy is calling me," I replied, indicating my cousin who was standing under the monkey bars, waving at me. He finally set me down, and I ran off, not looking back. That encounter started four years of sexual abuse from my

Steadfast Love

grandpa, where he lavished extra attention, gifts, praise and affection on me.

When I was 8, my aunt came over to visit. "I understand Dad takes care of Kristi quite a bit," she mentioned to my mom, sipping from her coffee cup.

"Yes, he's been great. I've had my hands full, and he's volunteered to take care of her," my mom answered.

"I don't think you should let Kristi stay with him anymore," my aunt replied, looking at her hands folded on the kitchen table.

My mom stared at her. "Why?"

"I didn't want to have to bring this up, but Dad has a problem." She paused. "When Mom and he were dating, he molested her sisters. When all of us girls were old enough, he turned his attentions to us and our friends. Now that we're older and have kids of our own, he's started molesting our girls. Kristi included."

Hiding around the corner in the dining room, I cringed against the wall. *The secret is out. Will Mom and Dad hate me? Am I not the only one? Grandpa told me I was special. Was he lying to me? Does he really love me? Will Mom and Dad still love me?* I thought.

"Kristi," my mom called to me.

I peeked around the corner. "Yeah," I whispered.

"Come here please," she ordered. I walked into the kitchen and stood between her and my aunt. "Is your aunt telling me the truth? Has Grandpa been touching you and doing things that he shouldn't with you?" she asked.

Looking down at my feet, I couldn't squeeze any

This Could Be You

sound out of my mouth. I nodded.

My mom leaned back in her chair and sighed. The room was quiet, and I continued to stare down at my feet. *Is she disappointed in me? Does she hate me? Why isn't she saying anything?* I asked myself.

"We're going to your dad's work. I want you to talk to some of his female co-workers," she told me, standing and pushing her chair away. She looked at my aunt. "Thank you for telling me."

The ride to the police station was quiet, the only sound in the car coming from the radio. When we arrived, Mom directed me to a sexual abuse investigator. She took me into a private room to talk while Mom went to look for my dad.

"Can you point out where your grandpa touched you?" the lady police officer asked, pulling out an anatomically correct doll. I pointed out the places Grandpa touched me. "Where did he ask you to touch him?" Again, I pointed to the places. Over the next three hours, I told her my story. After she finished questioning me, she called my sister into the room and asked her similar questions.

"Grandpa touches me in my underwear," my sister told her.

"Did you tell anyone?" she asked.

"I told Mommy and Daddy," she responded.

The tall, dark-haired police officer nodded and then called my parents into the room. "I've questioned both girls, and their stories are similar." She looked at my father, sitting in the chair in his uniform. "Your father has been abusing these girls. Kristi for quite some time." My dad sobbed into his

Steadfast Love

hands, and my mom sat there, stunned. "Did you have any idea? Beth said that she told you he touched her in her underpants? Did she?" the officer questioned.

"She told us a few months ago," my dad stuttered. "I talked to my sisters about it, but they told me that I shouldn't be concerned, so I didn't take her seriously. Now I wish I had," he said guiltily.

"We'll have to press charges," the officer replied. "Would you like some time to talk to your mother before we go out to pick him up?" she asked my dad.

"Yeah, I'll go talk to her," my dad responded. "Why don't you take the girls home. I'll call my sisters, and we'll tell Mom together," he told my mom.

Mom took us home while Dad met with my aunts. I'm positive Grandma knew all along, but when Dad told her that her husband would be taken into custody for sexual abuse, she denied it. She denies it to this day, because she's still married to him.

Grandpa pled on lesser counts and was sentenced to counseling and hypnotherapy. I've only seen him once since then, when we happened to meet up at a doctor's appointment. Dad turned to alcohol instead of attending counseling. I hated counseling and drug my feet whenever I had to go.

Dad took an early retirement from the police force and moved us to Alaska. I was happy and complacent there for the six weeks we actually stayed. We didn't stay long because Mom and Dad's marriage started to fall apart. When I was 12, Mom and Dad divorced. However, they continued to get back

This Could Be You

together — not dating to see if they could work their problems out, but gung ho, moving back in with each other. It never worked out. Dad and Mom fought, and Mom would pack us up and move back in with her parents. This cycle occurred for four years. Then it finally ended.

"You're drunk again," my mom snarled at my dad, as he stumbled in the front door at 9 p.m.

"Yeah, I am. What of it?" he retorted.

"I'm tired of you coming home late and drunk to boot! The kids are going to bed, and you never spend any time with them," she remarked.

I walked into the room from the bathroom, having brushed my teeth. "Goodnight, Mom. Goodnight, Dad," I told them.

"Night, sweetie," my dad replied.

"Goodnight," my mom announced before turning her attention back to my dad. "We don't have enough money for you to be spending it on alcohol every night."

"We're not married anymore. It's not our money, it's my money, and if I want to spend it on alcohol, then I will," my dad snapped.

"Why do you insist on drinking so much? You never spend time at home or with the kids."

"I like to relax after work, and I know I can't do it here because you're always yelling at me. It reminds me why we got divorced in the first place."

"That may be the case, but you still get back together with me," she returned.

"You don't need to remind me. You're here, aren't you?" he said sarcastically.

Steadfast Love

"I don't have to be. I can take the kids out of here tonight so you can have your privacy and a place to relax. Just say the word go and we're gone."

"Don't tempt me."

"Oh no, please tell me to leave. Tell me you want me to snap up your children in the middle of the night and take them out of here. You don't spend time with them anyhow."

"I'm their father, not their best friend. You treat them like they're your friends and not your children. You need to act like a parent, not a buddy," he commented.

"All you want to do is discipline them. You don't care how they feel," she rebutted.

"I act like their father."

"You act like the drunk that you are!" she yelled.

"Get out. What did you want me to say? Oh, yeah, GO. This is it. I can't take this maybe we will, maybe we won't stay together cycle we're in. Let's say we tried it. Many times. It's not going to work out. Take the kids and run back to your parents, like you always do," he raged.

"Fine. We're out of here," she replied, storming down the hall and pounding on our doors. "Get up! Get dressed. We're leaving and going to Grandma and Grandpa's," she called through my door. I got up, peeling my pajamas over my head, still dressed underneath. I always knew when the fighting escalated that quickly that we'd soon be headed back to Grandma's. We had done it often the last four years. Only this time was the last time. True to his word, Dad moved on, never taking Mom back. When I was

This Could Be You

17 and almost out of high school, Dad married again and quit drinking entirely. Mom waited another 17 years before getting remarried, maybe in the hopes that Dad would take her back.

After high school, I moved to New Jersey to become a nanny. In October, after three months of being very homesick, I moved back to Centralia, Washington. I shared a little apartment with my friend's ex-fiancé, Shannon, attended the local community college and worked for a factory outlet store.

One evening, in early November, I went to pick up my friend from Kentucky Fried Chicken where she worked. Parked in the back in my Honda Prelude, with my new perm, I waited and watched a young man come out the back door, carrying a bag of trash. After dumping it in the dumpster, he walked over to my car.

"What are you doing here?" he asked me.

"Waiting for my friend. She gets off at 11," I replied. "Why?"

"We've had some cars broken into lately, and I wanted to see why you were sitting back here in your car," he responded.

"Do I really look like a threat?" I asked facetiously. "What are you, the parking lot patrol?"

"Yeah, I guess I am," he replied with a smile. We started dating the next week.

On December 5, 1991, a construction company was working on putting in a sewer line in the alley behind our apartment, when they broke the gas line. Our neighbors smelled the gas so they called the fire department. When the firefighters came, they told us

Steadfast Love

that they smelled the gas but then didn't call the gas company to have them correct the problem. Believing that we had already done what we could do, we went back to our apartment. I slept on a daybed in our living room, giving Shannon the only bedroom in our one-bedroom apartment.

"I don't have to go to work until late tomorrow morning. It's the first day to sell Christmas trees, so I'll be able to sleep in," he informed me before heading to bed.

"I get to sleep in, too. I don't have to work tomorrow at all," I told him, snuggling down under my covers, lying on my right side.

"Goodnight. I'll try to be quiet in the morning, if I'm up before you," he announced.

"Night," I murmured, the warmth of the covers already making me drowsy.

The next morning, I heard Shannon moving around, but continued to lay with my eyes closed, savoring those last minutes before fully coming awake and starting my day. My arm felt chilled in the room, having come out of the covers overnight, but it felt so heavy when I tried to move it underneath again, so I left it.

BOOM! The bathroom door slammed shut, a towel wedged in it. The roof exploded, catapulting four feet in the air, and a ball of flames blazed through the kitchen, dining room and over the left side of my body where I slept in the living room. Though the front door was right in front of me, I jumped up from bed and headed towards the bright light, a hole in what had been the dining room wall.

This Could Be You

Jumping through the wall, I landed in the cold grass. *Oh, that feels so good. So cool,* I thought. I heard screams of pain and horror. *Who's screaming?* I wondered, not realizing that the high-pitched shrieks were coming from my mouth. I stumbled across the street, falling to the curb. I looked at the flames shooting from the sides of my apartment and saw my neighbors coming down the stairs, carrying their baby. *Good, they're okay,* I thought. My eyes started to swell shut, and I had difficulty seeing the hustle of firefighters striving to put out the fire and the neighbors, who were insuring everyone was safe. I glanced down at my hands, surprised to see them white and my skin flaking off.

"Everything is okay. The firefighters are working on getting the flames out before they spread. I'm here with you," a lady consoled me, patting my head. "Someone's bringing some ice to dump on you to cool the burns."

I nodded. *I'll have to tell sis that I was in a fight. She'll think that's cool,* I thought, feeling my eyes swell more. *They must look like someone punched me.* Someone dumped ice over my body. I shivered and started to shake.

"I think she's in shock," I heard someone shout. "Where's the ambulance?"

"They're on their way," another disjointed voice called.

"The ambulance will be here soon. They'll take care of you. Hang in there," the lady, still patting my head, consoled me.

"I have to go to the bathroom," I whispered to

Steadfast Love

her.

"That's okay. You can go right here. No one will know," she assured me.

"I can't go here. Not with people running around," I whispered, determined to hold it in, even though the early morning urge to pee would not go away.

I heard sirens and the screech of tires. "The ambulance is here," she announced. I felt hands touching me, soothing me and then lifting me.

"Let's get her in the ambulance. I'll get him stabilized, and they can ride together," the paramedic commanded. The other paramedic led me to the ambulance. I sat down on the stretcher, waiting as they brought Shannon to the ambulance. "Lie down, miss," the young man requested, gently pressing me down. I closed my eyes, feeling numbness and pain at the same time. My mind was a jumble of thoughts, and I just wanted to sleep to escape the pain.

"Kristi, are you okay?" someone called to me. I opened my eyes to see my grandparents' friend, Marlene, standing at the back of the rig, anxiously looking in at me.

"I don't know. I think so," I replied. "Could you let my family know?"

"I'll call them."

"Ma'am, we need to get moving," the paramedic told Marlene, having loaded Shannon and trying to close the doors.

"Is she going to be okay?" she asked him.

"I don't know," I heard him say before the doors slammed shut.

This Could Be You

The ride to the hospital was chaotic as the paramedics worked on Shannon and me, trying to assess the burns and relieve any discomfort we were feeling. Once we arrived at the emergency room, Shannon and I were rolled into the same examination room, and nurses and doctors bustled around. "We'll have to send them to Harborview for them to assess these burns," a doctor mentioned, referring to the hospital in Seattle and marking my chart.

I did not realize how bad my burns were. 42 percent of my body had second and third degree burns. Though Shannon, who had lit the cigarette that started the explosion of built up gas under the bathroom floor, had 60 percent of his body burned, he was very hairy and only had first and second degree burns. "Someone is here to see you," the intensive care nurse told me.

"Who is it?" I asked. She mentioned an old friend. "Oh, I haven't seen them in a while. Send them back."

Shad visited often. "Nice hair," he commented the first time he saw me, referring to my perm sticking straight up out of the bandages that covered my head.

"I try to look my best when I see you," I joked back, happy that he wasn't repulsed by my burns. I felt monstrous. When looking at different parts of my face and arms, one could see the different layers of skin, depending on the depth and severity of the burn. Still being in the early stages of our relationship, and vain at the age of 18, I didn't like having him see me that way.

Steadfast Love

My days in ICU numbered 10. Twice a day, the nurse would debride me, scrubbing my dead, burned skin off to improve healing of the good tissue. My nerves started to heal, their endings having been burned off. Anything — especially air — that touched my nerves created excruciating pain. My bones hurt, and it felt as though my skin would fall off. They moved me out of ICU when I had my first grafting surgery. They removed skin from my butt, transplanting it to my left hand. Gluing hooks to my nails, they stretched my hand out onto a device that looked like a wire tennis racquet called a Ukulele splint that held my hand immobile. After surgery, my debriding went from twice a day to once a day.

I had one roommate, Angel, whose pastor visited her. "May I pray for you?" he asked me on one of his visits.

"Sure," I told him, not knowing what to expect since no one had ever prayed for me before. He prayed for healing of my burns, relief from my pain and peace in my heart and mind. I felt a great sense of peace flood over me, and I knew God would make everything okay. *How can I know God will make everything okay? I've never had any relationship with him. I don't even know who he is,* I thought. But for some reason, I knew he would make everything okay.

I spent Christmas in the hospital and recovered there for a total of four weeks. Then I moved in with my mom's parents. Grandma took care of me, debriding me daily and changing my bandages. When I was 19, and Shad only 17, we moved in together. He assumed the responsibility of treating my burns.

This Could Be You

Relying on him that way and familial disapproval of our moving in with each other created turmoil in our relationship. After two years, the construction company settled.

"Let's use your settlement money to move to Bellingham," Shad suggested, referring to a town three hours north.

"Okay," I agreed, hoping to escape the turmoil our relationship endured by new surroundings.

In 1995, Shad asked me to marry him. I shouted yes. Deciding to get married in Olympia because it was more convenient for our families, we had a difficult time finding a place to marry us. The churches wouldn't agree because we were living together, didn't attend church and hadn't been baptized. Finally, a Lutheran pastor agreed. "I'll marry you, but you'll have to go through premarital counseling and go through confirmation."

"We'll do it," we promised. We went through the classes for confirmation, and as I learned about God and his love, I felt the peace that I had experienced in the hospital when Angel's pastor prayed over me. I felt a presence that I had never encountered before. *I am the answer; turn to me*, God told me. *I have wonderful plans for you. Trust me and turn to me.* I trusted him, and the peace of knowing him filled me. *I will always be with you*, he promised.

After our wedding, we settled down into married life in Bellingham. Shad continued to travel for work, and I started a new job where I met Tiffany. We walked together in the evenings after work, and I found a Christian friend that supported me when I

Steadfast Love

felt lonely. I discovered that I was pregnant. I had a smooth pregnancy, just some morning sickness, and all my checkups showed up fine.

"We'll have to induce you if you don't start to have contractions by Thursday," my doctor informed me. "Your insurance deductible rolls over on Monday, right?"

"Yes."

"We want you to have this baby before that rollover occurs," she told me.

Thursday came and they induced me. I chatted with the nurses, then the pills took effect, and I became very uncomfortable. After many hours, I changed positions continually but with no progress. "How's it going in here?" a nurse asked, coming into the room where I was lying in the tub, going through a contraction and almost throwing up. I looked at Shad, one eye open and glinting.

"Don't ask," he commented for me, knowing that I really wanted to tell her just to get out of the room.

Finally, I delivered a beautiful seven-pound, six-ounce girl. She was perfect. However, because of the extreme labor, my uterus didn't contract, and the doctor and nurses had a bloody mess on their hands.

"Go over and see our little girl," I told Shad, not realizing how much I was bleeding.

"No, I'll stay right here for now. The nurses are taking care of her," he replied, holding onto my hand and maintaining the calm he has always had in any crisis.

"Your uterus is enlarged, but the bleeding has stopped," the doctor assured me.

This Could Be You

"Can I see my daughter now?" I asked.

"Yes, they're almost finished cleaning her up. What are you going to name her?"

"Allison," I told her.

The nurse laid my perfect little girl in my arms. "Oh, Shad, isn't she beautiful?"

"Yes, she is," he agreed, beaming.

We took our little girl home, just a little jaundiced. Shad was home for a couple of weeks before he had to travel again for work. At her six-week checkup, I took her in. She was happy and still as perfect as the day she was born.

"You're going to need to take Allison to the children's hospital emergency room. Ask for the gastroenterologist," her pediatrician surprised me by announcing.

"What?" I asked in disbelief. "What could be wrong with her? And what's a gastroenterologist?"

"Gastroenterologists specialize in studying the digestive system and its disorders. Allison's jaundice concerns me, and I want to make sure that something isn't wrong with her liver," the pediatrician stated.

Gathering the diaper bag, I carried Allison out to the car and drove to the children's hospital. Arriving at the ER, they admitted her for testing. Since Shad was unreachable, and knowing he would call that evening like he did every night, I changed the outgoing message on our answering machine, telling him to call my cell phone instead.

Shad called. "They're admitting Allison for tests at the children's hospital. Her pediatrician was con-

Steadfast Love

cerned about her jaundice," I informed him.

"I'll be home as soon as I can," he assured me.

After a very long night, not getting much sleep and walking the floor with a very hungry Allison, I was exhausted and ready to give up. Allison kept crying, telling me she was hungry. But I couldn't feed her because she had to have an empty stomach for her tests. Walking up and down the hall, trying to soothe her crying, nothing worked. *Oh, Lord, I can't do this anymore. Allison won't stop crying, and I don't know what to do. Help,* I prayed.

"Can I help?" a woman asked, approaching me wearing a suit and a hospital badge.

"Yeah, could you please take her? I can't walk her anymore, and they haven't come to take her for tests yet," I responded.

I handed my baby to a complete stranger. She started to walk up and down the hall with her. "Find a place to sit down and rest," she told me.

I searched for a place, dropping into the first seat I found. *Thank you, Lord,* I prayed, recognizing that this woman was sent in answer to my cry for help.

Finally, they came to take her for her tests, and I thanked the woman for her help. "My pleasure," she answered, disappearing down the hall.

By the time Dr. Christie had the test results, Shad had arrived. "Everything is elevated in all of her liver tests. That can mean one of two things. Biliary atresia or neonatal hepatitis. We won't know for certain which it is until we can do exploratory surgery."

"What do those mean?" Shad asked. "What is the difference between the two?"

This Could Be You

"Biliary atresia is a progressive inflammatory process that begins soon after birth. It is when the network of tubular ducts that drain bile from the liver to the small intestine gets blocked or disappears. In essence, the immune system sees the bile ducts as an enemy and they shut down. Biliary atresia occurs in one of 15,000 births. It is not hereditary, not contagious, not preventable and affects only newborns. The preferred treatment is to perform a surgical procedure called the Kasai procedure. The small intestine is attached directly to the liver where bile is expected to drain. There is a 25 percent chance that she would need the Kasai only. Otherwise, she will have to have a liver transplant.

"Neonatal hepatitis is an inflammation of the liver that occurs only one or two months after birth. The infant usually has jaundice, doesn't gain weight or grow normally and can't absorb vitamins. If she does have neonatal hepatitis, then there is a risk of infection to the brain which could cause mental retardation or cerebral palsy. We can give her vitamin supplements and medication to help excrete bile from the liver. However, we won't know which it might be until we do exploratory surgery."

"I don't want my baby to die," I cried out. Shad put his arm around me, and I leaned my head on his shoulder, sobbing.

"I'll schedule Allison's surgery," Dr. Christie announced, leaving the room.

Allison's surgery revealed biliary atresia, and they performed the Kasai procedure. She stayed in the hospital for 10 days, and then we brought her

Steadfast Love

home. Her once perfect skin now revealed a scar from her side clear across her ribcage. I started charts to help us keep track of her medications, and Shad stayed home for a while before he had to go back to work, leaving me to take care of Allison.

    I started to attend church again, having stopped after getting pregnant and life getting so busy. Tiffany's church prayed for strength for me and healing for Allison. Both Shad and my families were supporters on the surface, but naysayers in the end, discussing Allison's death and not believing that she would get better. The support of my church family and their prayers kept me going when I felt like giving up. God was always there, next to me, being my strength and helping me through every day. When I felt I couldn't go on, he would send someone my way to help take care of Allison or just pray with me. I always felt better.

    "The Kasai procedure provided a clear pathway from her liver to her small intestine, but she's developed cholangitis, a bacterial infection of the bile duct," Dr. Christie informed me on one of her checkups. "We'll admit her and get an IV antibiotic going on her to hit the infection quickly. She also has ascites — fluid has accumulated in her stomach. We can treat it with diuretic medication, or we may possibly need to drain it."

    The IV antibiotic worked, and her cholangitis cleared up. I was able to take her home. Her first Christmas was fast approaching. "Can you believe Christmas is almost here?" I mentioned to Shad one evening. "When we had Allison, this was not how I

This Could Be You

expected to be celebrating her first Christmas."

"Yeah, but she's here with us. That's what matters."

"I agree." I got up from the couch and went to check on her. "Shad, come quickly," I called.

"What is it?" he asked, coming into the nursery.

"She hasn't been able to keep anything down today," I told him, indicating the mess that Allison had just vomited.

We took her to the children's hospital, where they admitted her for more testing. It was December 22, 2000.

"I didn't want to, but I think we should put a nasogastric tube (NG tube) in her," I commented, referring to the tube inserted through the nose, down the esophagus and into the stomach to put substances and nutrients in her body.

They inserted the tube, but she incessantly vomited whatever the hospital put into her. After more tests, they discovered that she had pancreatitis brought on by all of her medications. They took her off of all liquids and food to get the pancreas back in line. She spent her first Christmas in the hospital. After six days, her numbers were fine, so they started to feed her again. She threw up again.

After being in the hospital for two and a half weeks and having TPN, a combination of lipids and sucrose that was difficult for the liver to process, Dr. Christie announced, "We're going to do some upper and lower GI tests to see why she can't keep anything down."

"The tests revealed a spider web like adhesion on

Steadfast Love

the abdomen, attached to the bowels and creating a kink. We'll have to go into surgery to correct it," he told us. However, before she could get in for surgery, she contracted respiratory syncytial virus (RSV), a bronchial virus, from someone at the hospital. It took her two weeks to get over that, only to come down with Para influenza, an upper and lower respiratory infection.

"I feel like she just gets over one sickness, only to contract another one," I complained to Shad.

"I know. I don't remember a day when she wasn't sick," he remarked.

I nodded and looked down at her sleeping in the crib. I noticed that her arm around the pic line, the implant that had four or five ports for easy access to her veins without sticking her with a needle, was turning red.

"She has a yeast infection in her blood from the pic line. We'll give her amphotericin B to clear up the infection," the doctor told us.

Once her viruses were gone, and she was over the yeast infection, she went into surgery to correct the adhesion. She came back from surgery with her belly nice and flat since they had also drained her stomach. I sat down in the rocking chair and held her close, enjoying her warmth. She snuggled close to me, burrowing her head into my neck and taking my hair in her little fingers, twirling and smoothing it.

"You go ahead to the room at Kid's Village," Shad told me. "I'll stay with her tonight."

At 8:30 the next morning, he called me. "Are you going to be much longer?"

This Could Be You

"Not long, why?"

"She's having some complications. You should get over here."

"I'll be there as soon as I can." I hung up and rushed around getting ready.

When I arrived at Allison's room, it was full of people and activity. "Her pneumonia levels are high, and her kidneys aren't functioning," Shad told me. "They're going to give her an enema. I'm supposed to go down later this morning for tests. Allison has been moved up to Status One on the transplant list, and they need to see if I'm a match."

The doctors started to scramble around Allison. "You need to get out of here," one nurse told us and started to push us out of the ICU room. "You need to leave now," she said when Shad started to balk at leaving.

When we were allowed back in, I noticed that they had to put her on a respirator. "Her blood vessels were enlarged as a result of the surgery. They ruptured and started to bleed. We had to put a balloon in her throat to expand her breathing tube." Dr. Christie looked at us solemnly. "I don't think Allison is going to live much longer."

Her kidneys started to shut down, so they put her on dialysis. However, her blood clotted, not allowing the dialysis to work. Unfortunately, they couldn't give her heparin because they didn't want to thin the blood too much.

A nurse called Shad and I from the ICU sleeping room at 4 a.m. "Her pupils are no longer reacting. We'll have to do an MRI on her, but the specialist

Steadfast Love

doesn't come in until 6 a.m."

"Then call him," I demanded.

The specialist arrived at 5:15 a.m. The nurses bagged Allison so she could go to the MRI room.

Shad went into the viewing room with the doctor, while I accompanied Allison and the nurse into the room. The MRI machine sat in the middle of the room, stickers decorating the inside edges, with walking room around the perimeter. The nurse put Allison on the machine, and it started to whir. As Allison started to go through, nausea welled up inside me, and I walked over to the sink, feeling as though I would throw up. My knees got weak, and I leaned against the counter. After the test, Shad walked into the room and came over to me. "She's gone. The doctor said he's never seen that severe of a brain bleed in an infant before." I leaned against him in shock.

Back in her room, they placed her back on the respirator. Her chest rose and fell with every beep of the machine. I called Tiffany, asking her to call our families to come. I had no desire to talk to my family, resentful that they never visited her when she was sick but would be coming shortly when she was dying. I held her, her heavy body now full of fluids again, and Shad read *Guess How Much I Love You* to her. At 3 p.m., we took her off of the machines. I prepared myself, wondering if she would turn blue. She took three last breaths, and then she was gone.

I laid her back on the bed. "I have to leave. There's no reason for me to stay here anymore. She's not here," I sobbed.

This Could Be You

Shad and I exited the room, walking down to the waiting room to let the family know she was gone. Moving on to the chapel, where Tiffany and her family were praying, we said our goodbyes to them. Shad carried her car seat, and I carried her little suitcase out of the hospital.

I want a car to come and run me over. I don't want to finish crossing this parking lot. Not without Allison. It feels so wrong to be leaving here without her. Please, let a car just run me over now, I thought.

We decided to have the memorial service in Olympia to accommodate the rest of the family. When we arrived at the hotel, I pulled out the phone book from the desk drawer. Searching through the yellow pages, I couldn't believe I was looking for a funeral home. Shad's mom came with us as we went to funeral homes.

"Now, these baby urns are so cute. They look like little salt and pepper shakers," one lady said. "There's not much left of babies after they are cremated."

"I don't care. I don't want to know that," I raged, throwing my hands up in the air, turning and walking away. "I can't deal with this."

We ended up getting an adult-sized urn for Allison. "She was little, but she'll always be big in my eyes," I told Shad. We had the memorial catered.

"Why don't you go to Costco and get some meat and cheese and cut it up yourself?" my dad asked.

"Dad, my daughter just died. I'm not going to cut up meat," I argued.

We stayed for three days after the memorial be-

Steadfast Love

fore returning home. A couple of months later, my mom's dad died, leaving my grandma with no one to take care of her. We sold our house in Bellingham and moved back to Centralia, buying my grandparents' farm.

We visited Destiny Christian Center on Father's Day. Pastor Bill's message of a father's love was powerful, but our loss was still so fresh that we ended up not going back because we couldn't cope. I wanted to go to a church where I could get fed and refilled every Sunday and not get involved in church activities. I wanted a comfortable church where I could heal from my loss.

"I'm ready to have another baby. I don't want it to be just the two of us," I told Shad not long after moving back.

"I agree. I want another one, too."

When the ultrasound showed twins, I know God was blessing us for not giving up when it got hard watching Allison suffer and die. I know God protected me from finding out too early that I was having twins because I would have stressed over the high-risk pregnancy. I had no issues during the rest of my pregnancy. In fact, once again, I had to be induced, this time at 37 weeks. With no complications, we welcomed Emily and Ashley into our world. Three years later, we welcomed Isaac, a male reminder of Allison because they look exactly alike.

Allison was sent to us for her tiny amount of time to wake us up to the acts against God in my family's history — my grandfather's sexual abuse, my dad's alcoholism, divorce and addictions. With our com-

This Could Be You

mitment to God, and through his guidance, our marriage is solidified. Though I was forgiven of my sins when we went through the confirmation, it wasn't until Allison was diagnosed that I become passionate about God. Without him to lean on, without his steadfast love supporting me daily, I would not have gotten through the daily struggles and fears. God is still faithful. The twins are a constant reminder that God was always there for me, and I know that he will always be there for me.

The Story of Laura
Written by Angela Prusia

Soft coos made my heart swell in an unfamiliar way. Is this what love was? I placed my daughter's tiny hands in mine and marveled at the perfection of someone so small. The nurse told me babies didn't smile on their own for several weeks, but I watched Jacquelin's lips curve upward.

"Look at you," I whispered. "Smiling already and proving the nurses wrong." I caressed her head, which was full of wisps of golden hair. "Mama loves you, baby girl."

Jacquelin's eyelids fluttered closed as she nestled close to me. I tucked the little hand that had escaped into the receiving blanket and watched my daughter's chest rise and fall in perfect rhythm. "Thank you, God," I whispered into the silence before I, too, fell asleep.

Jacquelin's cries woke me. "Hush, baby," I said as I fed her. "Mama's here."

An empty cafeteria tray lay on the table next to my bed. Diapers and baby clothes — gifts from my friends at church — were stacked next to my tattered suitcase, ready to go home. The women had also given me a crib and a sheet set with baby bumpers when they'd thrown me a shower a few weeks earlier.

I looked around the hospital room, wishing my husband had brought flowers or a balloon, anything to celebrate the birth of our first child. There was

This Could Be You

nothing.

A nurse knocked on the door. "You ready, child?" she asked, her voice gentle.

I couldn't look at her eyes. The pity I saw threatened to undo me.

"Do you have someone you can call?" she asked. "A friend? Any family?"

I looked at the door, knowing my husband would be too stoned to come. He'd been present for the birth; otherwise, I hadn't seen him for the entire week I'd been in the hospital. My mom wouldn't be coming for another week and a half. She couldn't change the flight she'd booked months ago. Who knew my daughter would arrive early?

I nodded, holding back the tears. The nurse seemed to sense my emotion. "I'll be back then."

I reached for the phone, forcing my voice to sound upbeat when I heard my friend's voice over the line. "Could you come get me and Jacquelin?"

"We'll be right there," Cindy said. She didn't mention my absent husband. She knew my desperation.

"Thanks," I managed to get out before I hung up. Of course, Cindy's husband, Tom, would come. I longed for such a strong relationship with my husband.

Hot tears stung my eyes. Disappointment mixed with my fear. What my husband didn't blow on alcohol and drugs, we used to scrape by with each month. I could barely take care of myself. How could I take care of someone so small?

My lips quivered as I kissed Jacquelin on the

The Story of Laura

head. "It's just you and me, little one."

When my mom arrived, she began to suspect the problems between me and my husband, but I pushed her questions aside. I didn't want to ruin our visit when our time together was so infrequent. Why worry her? We were separated by too many miles for her to do anything anyway.

After two and a half years of marriage, I was used to my husband's frequent absences. I was a young bride, but I tried to be a good wife. After work, I enjoyed cleaning house and fixing dinner for the two of us. Too often, though, I would eat our supper alone in front of the television.

My husband came from a wonderful family. He was one of the youngest of eight children of a pastor and his wife. When my high school friends and I were driving around one night and met him at a gas station, I couldn't believe my luck. I'd always felt like an only child since my brothers lived with my father, and I was never close to my stepfather's older children. My husband's family welcomed me as one of their own.

I saw marriage as a means of escape. For as long as I could remember, my stepfather singled me out for abuse. As a young child, I would awake to find myself without the pajamas I had gone to sleep in. As I got older, I was terrified to come home after school. Because my stepfather's day started early as a logger, he would often be home before my mother got off work. I would hide in my closet for hours, hoping he wouldn't find me. My stepfather touched me a lot. My mother heard the vulgar talk, but she

This Could Be You

denied the abuse. I couldn't blame her. Her life was hard growing up. She'd been raised by several different relatives and left home by the age of 16 or 17. After so many bad relationships, including one with a violent man who wanted to kill her, I know my mother wanted to believe the best about my stepfather.

The older I grew, the worse the abuse became. I tried to sleep at friends' houses or even with my stepsister because she had a lock on her door, but my stepfather got wise to my schemes. He would complain to my mother that I was gone too much. He even loosened the bolts on the lock on my stepsister's door. I lived in constant fear. I had no place of refuge. I couldn't shower without my stepfather coming into the bathroom. Even the hallway was an opportunity for him to press up against me. He constantly propositioned me to do things I hated. I was a lost little girl. Not until I turned 15 did I start to realize I could threaten my stepfather. Only when I said I would call the police did I see fear in his eyes.

I didn't understand boundaries, so I let many boyfriends take advantage of me. I fell for the flirting, thinking each relationship would fill the emptiness I felt inside. When I met my husband, I went to the church where his father preached. I knew they were different — people called them "holy rollers" — but I felt comfortable with them. That Easter Sunday was the first time I'd heard the gospel message. During the altar call, I gave my heart to God. The decision was life changing. I wanted to live a holy life, so I told my husband I didn't want to break God's

The Story of Laura

laws by sleeping with him anymore. My stepfather threatened to press statutory rape charges against him because of my age, so marriage seemed the only option.

I was not even 16, so I denied the warning signs. I overlooked his work as a DJ and bouncer at a bar and the marijuana sales he made to support his drug habit. He was six years older than me. In his teens, he almost died on the operating table during surgery on his appendix. His father placed the Bible on him, and he was healed. Not only did he struggle with the call of God placed on his life, he had unresolved issues from his childhood. Since his father had been an alcoholic before his life was transformed by Jesus, he harbored pain from those years. He rebelled, saying his father was too strict.

"Let's move, baby," he told me when he was laid off.

I didn't even hesitate. I could imagine the adventure we'd have together. We left Orofino, Idaho, for Noel, Missouri, more than 2,000 miles from home. One of my husband's sisters lived there and said there was work at a chicken plant. She even said we could live with her and her husband for a few weeks until we got established.

We both got jobs at the plant, working the swing shift. I didn't want to cut the chickens for fear I'd cut off a finger, so I packed the birds as they came down the conveyor belt. My husband drove the forklifts. Even though the factory was cold and windowless and the smell that surrounded the building made my stomach turn, I was grateful for the work.

This Could Be You

The adventure wasn't quite what I imagined. Over the next few years, we moved three more times. When we moved to the north side of Tulsa, Oklahoma, I was in for a big city education. We lived in the bad section of town, so I wasn't used to the prostitutes on the corner or the solicitations I received. I had to go from being a quiet, small-town girl to a loud spoken city girl who carried mace.

My husband partied constantly, often being gone for days at a time. I didn't understand his alcoholism, even when I witnessed him so drunk, he'd crawl to the toilet. Sometimes, he would take my car and leave me to walk home alone at night from work.

"Is this Laura?" I heard a voice ask over the phone one day.

"Yes," I answered. The hair on the back of my neck stood at the sound of the unfamiliar voice.

"You don't know me, but I'm the manager at the bar your husband goes to." I knew the place, even if I was too young to go there.

"What's wrong?" I managed to ask.

"Your husband is in jail," he said. "He was with a bunch of losers when they broke into a house."

I shouldn't have been surprised, but still the news hurt. I called my sister-in-law in nearby Miami, Oklahoma.

"I don't know what to do," I cried into the phone. The rental place that employed my husband included our rent.

"Hush," her voice soothed me over the phone. "Come live with us."

The Story of Laura

Three months later, he was out of jail. Sobered up, he vowed to change. "I've hit rock bottom," he said. "I'm gonna change, baby."

I was hesitant, but I wanted to make our marriage work. When he confessed his unfaithfulness, the pain was like a knife to my heart. All the times I waited for him, alone and afraid, he was out cheating on me.

"Can you forgive me?"

I swallowed the lump in my throat. Divorce wasn't an option. All the time my husband spent at the bar, I went to church. God had been working in my heart in a mighty way.

"Please," he asked again.

I nodded through my tears. "God, help me to love this man — my husband — despite my pain," I prayed silently. It wasn't long before I became pregnant with our daughter.

A friend at church tried to help him start a landscaping business, while the pastor became an accountability partner. The more he was confronted, however, the more he blamed others. Soon he slipped right back into his former lifestyle.

When my daughter was born, my heart was ready to become a mom, but he wasn't ready to accept the responsibility.

"I need money," he said shortly after our daughter's birth. His eyes — the pupils, small dots — told me he was stoned.

"We don't have any money," I said.

He started to rummage through the cabinets. "Where do you hide it?" he demanded. "I know

This Could Be You

your mom gave you some when she was here."

"Look at her." I pointed to our daughter. "I need things for the baby!" I screamed.

"I lost my job."

I wasn't surprised. Like always, he had no remorse. He simply changed clothes and left. Again.

Life wasn't easy, but God showed himself to me in mighty ways. He provided a loving home for my daughter while I worked. Her daycare worker went to church with me, so I was pleased with Jacquelin's care. I didn't have much, but I tithed what little I made. God proved faithful to his promise in Malachi. "'Bring the whole tithe into the storehouse... test me in this,' says the Lord Almighty, 'and see if I will not throw open the floodgates of heaven and pour out so much blessing that you will not have room enough for it.'" More than once, people from church would invite me over for supper or bring food and formula to me.

I never wanted to divorce my husband, and I prayed to God to restore our marriage. I started to lock the door at night when he wouldn't come home. My daughter and I couldn't live with the turmoil his lifestyle brought. He would pound on the door and yell with no regard for my sleeping child or for the neighbors. He expected to come into my bed when he returned, and when I wouldn't agree, he would get angry. One of those nights when he forced sex, I got pregnant with our son. I put his stuff outside of our apartment and kicked him out. I shouldn't have been surprised, but he moved in with another girl and got her pregnant. Two weeks after my son was

The Story of Laura

born, I served him divorce papers. He was in jail again, so he didn't contest anything. My heart was broken; he seemed indifferent.

Six years after moving away from home, I moved back to Doty, Washington, to be near the only family I knew — my husband's family. I rented a double-wide trailer 300 feet from his parents' house and the church where his father was still a pastor. I talked on the phone with my mom, but my stepfather had not changed. I would not let him near my children, especially my daughter. I was 24 when I told my mother about the abuse I'd endured as a child. She was crushed.

I went to school to become a teacher, but my young children made studying difficult. I changed direction so I could finish school sooner and became a medical office assistant. I wanted a good job so I could provide for my children.

I continued going to church and getting filled with God's word. At a volleyball game with the singles group from church, I met my second husband. Unfortunately, I didn't see the "wolf in sheep's clothing." I ignored a warning from my ex-husband's brother. He had a vision of me in a women's shelter, but I dismissed it.

My second husband was abusive, both verbally and physically. Since we moved to the country outside Centralia, and I had no car, I felt isolated. He was extremely strict and controlling especially in the way he wanted the house to be kept. Whenever he would yell at me about my housekeeping, my daughter would overcompensate and help me clean.

This Could Be You

My son, John, would sob in my arms.

I became pregnant in our first month of marriage. When my son, Jamie, was 9 weeks old, I awoke from a sound sleep to find him limp and unresponsive in his crib. I had a difficult time waking up my husband because he worked long days in the paper mill and slept with earplugs.

Jamie was in a coma by the time we arrived at the hospital. The doctors treated him for spinal meningitis because they couldn't diagnose his condition, other than to say his white blood count was high. My husband had a child from another marriage who had died from SIDS, so I was overwhelmed with gratitude to God when Jamie came out of his coma. If God hadn't woken me, my son would not have lived.

Three kids kept me busy, especially since Jamie had some brain damage and took medication for seizures. The doctors encouraged us to pursue early intervention therapy with Jamie, so my days were filled with physical therapy and speech appointments. An occupational therapist also made home visits. I was never so exhausted in my life.

My fourth pregnancy was forced. Because I was still nursing Jamie at night, I wasn't taking birth control. When my husband approached me, I cried, begging him to reconsider. I loved my children, but I couldn't handle an infant with the extra attention Jamie, now a year old, needed. He didn't care.

During my prenatal visits, the doctor asked me about my bruises, but I lied. A friend gave me a key to her house, in case I ever needed it. Even my pastor

The Story of Laura

from Full Gospel Lighthouse Church — a woman who treated me like her daughter — began to suspect the abuse. Her frequent calls angered my husband. Once, he even ripped the phone off the wall. My pastor's voice came over the line. "Laura, Laura, are you okay? Laura, Laura?" I couldn't leave without all of my children, and he made sure I was never alone with all four of them.

My older two children had no choice but to live with my husband's rage. The simplest of things would set him off: putting on jackets too slow, leaving a toy in the middle of the room, things that children do. I tried to ward off the abuse, but whenever I would have to leave for one of Jamie's appointments or my prenatal visits, I would come home to tear-stained faces. When I asked my children what happened, Jacquelin would say, "I can't tell you. Daddy will get mad." My hands would shake as memories of my stepfather's abuse would wash over me in waves. How many times had I heard the same words from my stepfather? I felt so powerless.

Child protective services got involved when the nurse at Jacquelin's school called to report welts on my daughter's legs from where my husband took a switch to her.

"You know you can lose Jacquelin," the child protection officer told me at work.

My heart hammered in my chest.

"And the other three children, too." His eyes bore into mine. "Everything depends on your response to me right now."

I poured out my heart and planned our escape. A

This Could Be You

few days later, on Halloween, I loaded the kids into the vehicle.

"Where are you going?" my husband asked as he came outside.

"Two of the kids have dentist appointments," I said, as I breathed a silent prayer for strength.

Jamie started to fuss about his car seat, and my husband came unglued. I walked to the side of the car and helped my son. My husband slammed the door in exasperation and huffed into the house.

I let out a sigh as I patted my purse. The only reason I had the checkbook was because we needed gas. I drove my kids to a women's shelter — just like in the vision — where we lived for a month. I left everything behind, including my job. Only my pastor knew where we stayed. The shelter helped me find low-income housing and assisted me with legal issues so I could divorce my husband. When he stalked me, I got a restraining order. When he violated that, he was jailed.

The next 12 years were years of healing. I took co-dependency classes and saw a counselor. Being a single mother was hard, but I rested on God's strength. Alone to raise four children, I had to rely on him. Gently, God walked me through depression and fear. Even though I had been hurt so much, he showed me that there was no freedom in fearing people. My guilt over what I'd put my children through was a burden for many years. I was on my knees constantly, praying on behalf of them.

It was hard to leave Full Gospel Lighthouse Church, but change was necessary for my kids.

The Story of Laura

When I drove by Destiny Christian Center, God nudged my spirit. My kids thrived in the youth group, and soon, we considered the church our family. I don't know what I would've done without the support of my brothers and sisters in Christ, especially with all the challenges of raising my four children. I was fearful to get too close to people, but the friendships I developed with different church members have been a balm to me. The teaching of God's word brought strength and comfort to me when I needed help the most.

I doubted I would ever marry again, but at age 40, I found a wonderful man, and we were married. Two years later, I can say I am in a healthy relationship. I am in love — something I questioned would ever happen.

I marvel at the strength of character in my children. All four of them know Jesus died for their sins and have accepted him into their hearts. Jacquelin challenged me in her teen years, but her heart changed at a youth camp. I am amazed at her sensitivity to those less fortunate. Both she and her brother, John, enrolled in a discipleship program when they graduated from high school. John is gifted with discernment and is a rock, unwavering in his passion to follow Christ. My youngest boys are in high school with bright dreams for their futures.

One of my favorite verses is found in Joel 2:25-27. "I will repay you for the years the locusts have eaten... You will have plenty to eat, until you are full, and you will praise the name of the Lord your God, who has worked wonders for you... Then you will

This Could Be You

know… that I am the Lord your God, and that there is no other; never again will my people be shamed."

I am living proof that God is a God of restoration. He has restored to me the years the locusts have eaten. I see my children, and I know God has worked wonders; he alone has broken the cycle of abuse. God has always been by my side. He has restored my confidence and given me peace. Never again will I be shamed.

Second Chance Drifter
The Story of Kevin Emerson
Written by Richard Drebert

The crystal meth clawed at my nerves like starving stray cats in a cage. My guitar soaked up my tremors as I choked the neck, strumming a throbbing, euphoric rhythm. I perched on an oak stool, flanked by a jerry-rigged amplifier, crooning my signature song, "Barstool Country," watching the performer aping in the dirty mirror across the bar. The man *still* enchanted me, his cadaverous face a contorted, animated blur. The man in the mirror was me.

Barstool country, it ain't never gonna die. Barstool country will always be alive. 'Cause I play it every night, and you know I play it right.

My scuffed cowboy boots clomped to the wood floor as I slid from my perch, and like a priest blessing the dead, I waved a backhanded acknowledgment to tattered applause. I flipped shut my guitar case and grabbed up the handle, ignoring shadows crawling the room. My groupies lolled in vacant chairs and roosted on the bar, screaming with wild acclaim — not for my voice or skill — my groupies exulted in my moral weakness.

I walked past a memory of myself taking shape in the mirror. A year ago, I dressed *sharp*, in tight Levis and leather boots. A Marlborough adorned my face with arrogance. Biceps stretched against a bright blue western-cut shirt, my muscles hard from swing-

This Could Be You

ing a hammer and hefting house beams. It was just a matter of time before the Fates tossed a record label or a Grand Ole Opry gig into handsome Kevin Singer's clever hands.

Then the jaunty image dissolved like steam, and an apparition issued from the streaky, beer-spattered glass. The western shirt hung on my shoulders like a faded blue tarp flung over a half-framed wall. A Marlborough butt drooped from my sallow, meth-sunken face, and vacant eyes — pupils wide with paranoia — gaped back at me warily. My prospects for fame had long ago deserted me, leaving me a depressed slave to the hard drugs that I peddled to other addicts to finance my own habit. And like my meth and ecstasy clients, drug lust had worn me thin, too. Down from 180, my brittle scarecrow chassis carried 145 pounds these days.

But meth was my second place addiction. Almost a decade ago, I had chained myself to a burning lust for celebrity after losing faith in my mother's religion. Fame tantalized me like the taste of honey — I yearned to gorge on it. Like many blossoming artists, I emulated my country hall of fame mentors, indulging in booze, sexual gratification and drugs. My addictions branded me as a willing host for demons to cache guilt and fear inside my head, and I had no strength to close the honky-tonk portal I had opened to the spirit world.

Tonight, a bottomless despair yawed black at the edge of my boot steps as I headed home from the bar. I couldn't even *run* toward hell anymore — I stumbled — and inside my tiny apartment, I flopped

Second Chance Drifter

onto the unmade bed, striking up a flame to light a joint, assuring my "soft landing" after weeks of meth parties. In the thick darkness, I fingered a small bag of crystalline rocks in my pocket and sucked in calming marijuana fumes, fully aware that my unholy groupies kept vigil with me. *They might carry me to hell in my sleep,* I worried, my soul grappling for any lifeline to save me.

A Sunday school memory, as intense as an ice water plunge, suddenly scrubbed away a noxious score of "cheatin' hearts" songs tattooed to my brain: *Jesus loves me this I know, for the Bible tells me so.* I remembered a smiling Sunday school teacher patting a colorful cardboard figure of Jesus onto a felt board, and the *rightness* in this childhood memory delivered a dash of forgotten peace.

Little Sounds of Light

"Larry, toss up that two-by-four!" Mr. Johnson balanced like a circus clown, his big hammer dangling from a yellow leather apron. My stepdad flung the stick of wood — and Mr. Johnson dodged in the nick of time.

"God bless you, man, you missed me again!" My stepdad looked mortified, and on the next toss, Mr. Johnson snatched the two-by-four in midair.

"Tell Kay we'll have the shingles on before the next hurricane," he laughed, pointing toward the Florida ocean beach where major storms brewed two or three times a year.

Cinderblocks, like rows of gray-colored Lego

This Could Be You

bricks, held up the bare bones of a church roof, and Mama sat with the door to our old Ford opened, waving at the burly, tanned carpenters mincing atop the framed walls. To everyone outside our family, Mama was "Pastor Kay," lauded for her gifted preaching. Soon, her small congregation would fill our neighborhood with Pentecostal fervor and song, especially my sister, brother and me: The Sounds of Light Trio.

My siblings and I sat in the backseat of our Ford, frying like sardines in a can, impatiently waiting for my stepdad. Axes and picks for chopping up kudzu and scrub brush stuck out of the car trunk. Mama had promised us a bonfire tonight at the property where we would soon install our mobile home. She frowned at the hot dog buns in a grocery bag, squished between my brother and me, and smiled at my sister, Cassie, poring over a Dr. Seuss book.

Cassie had barely clung to life when she was born with spina bifida. Shiny steel braces with hinges and rivets chaffed Cassie's little bare legs. Gripping her heels, the contraptions ran up past her knees to strengthen sinews and muscles weakened after operations. Watching her miracle baby struggle hit Mama hard.

I was Cassie's champion, too, and often jumped to her defense when thoughtless kids teased her, but I learned to educate rather than swing fists at their ignorance. "You know what spina bifida is?" The question usually silenced the taunts for a few seconds. "My sister has a disease in the spinal cord that controls her muscles, and that's why she wears

Second Chance Drifter

braces." When it dawned upon Cassie's persecutors that she was human after all, they usually shrank to a manageable size, and the satisfaction in playing the heartstrings of a "crowd" made a permanent home in my young heart.

"Thank you, Sounds of Light Trio! These wonderful children belong to our Pastor Kay." The applause in our new church fed me, enchanting my spirit and bolstering my self-worth. My siblings and I stood like smiling prodigies in the beautiful new sanctuary that my family helped build, in the church where Mama preached three times a week. The deacons had evaporated with the red-velvet offering pouches, and Mama rose from her seat slowly, like a woman holding in an electrical charge.

I never thought much about it then, but few kids have ever seen their own mothers on the business side of a pulpit. At 5'4" and 170 pounds, with wavy brown hair parted dead center, Mama's brown eyes searched the faces in the assembly, then like a dove's wings, her Bible lilted open in her hands. She stood in bare feet, like an Old Testament prophetess lately back from a tryst with the Almighty, and the small congregation fell silent as she bowed for a moment. Then with fervor, Mama plowed up the hardpan so God's word could take seed. On the stage, Mama reached deep within herself to a place where God answered her own needs, and she preached with all her heart.

Some folks may have felt that we kids hindered God's "move of the Spirit" with our giggling and wiggling, but our new fellowship had no children's

This Could Be You

church in those days. It seemed that our spiritual hunger was ignored, so I slept or drew pictures while Mama's sermons went on and on. The gospel seeds fell all around me but never really took root in my heart. I got "saved" every so often, goaded by some visiting evangelist, but afterward, I tamped the soil of my heart hard again to keep out feelings of guilt.

***

Little ones to him belong, they are weak, but he is strong.

Being a boy again in my fitful dreams left a bittersweet taste, and I shook myself awake, glancing at my wristwatch. Two days and nights had passed. I despised waking up after partying with "crystal" — it was always a hellish experience. My tongue rasped like sandpaper against my cracked lips, and I searched my pockets for a smoke, then yawned wide like a boney hound and nearly passed out.

The corners of my mouth ripped back like the unhinged jaws of a snake. Blood streamed down my chin, and I overturned a chair as I stumbled to a mirror to assess the damage to my second greatest asset as a country singer — my "good looks." Crystal meth was sucking the very life from my skin, drop by drop. Shakily, I lit up a cigarette and then crushed out the ember in favor of a joint. The meth rocks in my pocket seemed a better choice, but my belly clamored for food, too. I had to eat *something*, if I could keep it down. Dabbing at the corners of my

Second Chance Drifter

mouth with a dishtowel, I opened the fridge a crack and then slammed it shut as sour smells (mingled with profound guilt) overpowered me.

This twisted notion to sacrifice my soul for country stardom had fastened on my heart *when?* I was nearing a sad end, and every fiber of my being cried out for help, but hadn't I squandered my last chance for God's mercy when I broke trust with Jesus months ago? Guilt smothered me as I sat down to collect my thoughts and memories.

Shooting Star

As a child, I never understood the reasons why Mama quit preaching, but my family's exodus from our little church bruised something deep in her soul. I blamed the church "Christians" for our family's pain, and a barb festered deep in my heart — bitterness. My outrage led me to believe that I was just as righteous as any hypocrite I had sung for as a little "sound of light," and when we moved to a new neighborhood, I explored all things off limits to a former preacher's kid. Verse by verse, I rewrote the soul-saving music my mama had tried to instill in my heart, and I deliberately found relationships far from the safety of my family's faith.

New appetites invaded my mind when I met Dennis, an outsider like me who lived nearby, and he too seemed fascinated by anything forbidden. At Dennis' house, MTV sweet-talked me late into the night, and pornography set its hook firmly in my brain as we pored over magazines hidden in the

This Could Be You

woods. I still attended a church with my family regularly, but by 15, I discovered that my heart had plenty of room for as much sin as I could stuff inside. When I turned 16, my battered little family suffered a divorce, and Mama, my brother, my sister and I moved again.

In a new part of Santa Rosa County, Florida, I carried books in the halls of an old country high school nestled between a peanut field and a cotton field, where people wore coveralls to basketball games and church. I was a prime candidate for an Afterschool Special. I had a mangled family, no friends, and I was searching for a way to be cool. So what does a teenager do in the Afterschool Special to win respect and date a cheerleader? He risks it all and fights a school bully who's older and bigger.

In my junior year, I punched out a bully (who himself had just fought the toughest guy in school), and somehow I pulled off a triumph. The cool clique in our tiny school opened wide, and by the time I was 17, I was going steady with a girl, setting records in pole vaulting and dreaming of a hoops scholarship.

Yet even after achieving my goals, I still couldn't shake off a haunting discontent. After graduation, I shuffled through memories of Mama kicking off her shoes and flaying the devil with her sermons, while the high heavenly voices of her children resonated in God's sanctuary. I had been truly happy when I sang as one of the little "sounds of light," and performing for a crowd still scratched the itch for approval that I craved. During the next few years, I worked to per-

Second Chance Drifter

fect my guitar playing, hoping to regain the harmony that I remembered as a child — nothing else seemed to fill my cavernous need.

By 20 years old, my mind soaked up country music like saddle soap in leather, and I seldom needed the words on a karaoke screen at local bars — I had memorized hundreds of western hits. Often talent scouts watched me discreetly from side tables, measuring crowd reaction, my voice quality and, of course, sex appeal. By day, I swung a hammer and ran a construction crew; by night, I rode the karaoke circuit, singing, smoking dope and hanging out with friends, waiting to be discovered.

My Skoal, George Strait persona never roused the crowd like a Garth Brooks trapeze act, but most people agreed that I was destined for a stage somewhere. And I knew I had found my stride when people cried when I sang. Playing the heartstrings of my audiences happened more and more often — even grown men sniffled in their ashtrays — and suddenly, my music was in demand.

I was 21 when I left karaoke to recast myself as country star Kevin Singer. I joined a band called Crossover, and we played at a small club where massive pine trees stood sentry in the parking lot. With total seating for 70 or 80 patrons, The Pines became the perfect testing ground for Crossover — a place to "get tight" (practice) so we wouldn't get slaughtered at a larger club. My singing as a child, watching Mama on stage, and caring for my sister had prepared me; I instinctively knew how to plug into the mood of a crowd.

This Could Be You

Our band had our sights set on Shooters, with a 400-plus seating capacity, and the place where talent hunters found new blood for their labels. I began to write my own songs, getting ready for a leap to fame. The Pines crowds grew to capacity, but Crossover turned out to be a transition, and I turned to singing solo. In those heady days, I teetered on the edge of a record signing. I was a "not-quite-famous" country artist who framed houses till Friday afternoon, then showered, shaved and stuffed holey socks into cowboy boots and rode out to a club. Somewhere during a break from singing, I'd toke a marijuana joint and end up falling into bed by dawn.

Like my country idols, I was a workin' man, staying true to my dream and singing because I loved it, whether I got paid or not. My heart was broken after my longtime love left me all alone, and I needed dope just to keep my hands from shaking. I was shackled inside a sad country song, and I believed that I was living free.

An ex-girlfriend helped me write the next verse to my sad song. "Kev, you gotta' try ecstasy. I tell you, it's the most fun you'll ever have."

I had been with Cherry long enough to trust her grasp of what fun was, so before shooting pool with some friends, I popped a pill. While six of us passed a joint around a circle, I suddenly "blew up" as the ecstasy hit my system.

"Where'd you get this stuff? This is the best weed I ever smoked! I tell you, this is heaven." And I was hooked.

Ecstasy made Budweiser taste like dew from the

Second Chance Drifter

gods. While on ecstasy, my voice stole resonance from country icons like George Jones, and I played guitar with a matchless finesse. I was invincible. Hard-drug junkies shouldered out my docile pothead friends, and I flavored the new music I composed with a fresh vulgarity — more insinuating and base. My gift of connecting with people flourished, and I sang what my "friends" wanted to hear.

My new poison enhanced the timbre of my voice to flow rich and deep, like currents running beneath ocean waves, and this drifter could do anything. I believed that I owned more than my audience — I owned a piece of truth. I was right when the whole world was wrong, living and loving with passion that crowned my future like a Florida sunset, brilliant, immense and endless. The crowd's applause reached inside me. I dipped my guitar — a measured oblation — and their appreciation touched my heart, stroking, soothing.

My big "break" came when one of the most exciting country groups in Florida, Yellow River Band, asked me to sing solos between their sets. Months later, at a crowded country fair after a roar of applause, their lead singer held up his hands, and the 2,000-plus audience fell silent. "Now meet the country boy who helped write this rodeo love song, 'Cowboy Up.' Kevin Singer!"

The country fans went berserk as I walked upon the glittering stage, and suddenly, the surreal moment seemed worth any cost: swinging a cold hammer to keep the bills paid; singing in smoky bars to keep my dream alive; even losing the woman I al-

This Could Be You

ways thought I would marry.

I was 24 years old and fired up for a career as a songwriter and singer, but fate remained stingy, and fame danced just out of my reach. I played my heart out at most every club in the Bible belt, my ego swelling on the hopes of a record signing, but depression dogged me in my sober moments between synthetic highs. I worked, and I despaired as my old ambitions consumed me. "Barstool Country" still played in my mind and needed to die, so that God could write a new song in my heart.

One day, Mama called to ask, "Do you want me to find a dentist for you?" I could barely think straight as doped up as I was. One of my wisdom teeth had abscessed, swelled and throbbed like a sledgehammer on sheet iron.

"Yeah, I guess you better," I said. I hated drills and tiny, sharp probes.

"Fine, I'll get you an appointment on Wednesday."

"Thanks, Mama."

"And you can go to church with me Wednesday night."

The hammer came down again, and I grudgingly gave in. "Okay. Make the appointment." Mama had me in the crosshairs, and I hadn't realized it. In fact, there was much about Mama that had escaped my notice while I had been pursuing my country star ambitions. She had changed.

After leaving our family's church in Milton, Florida, Pastor Kay had struggled with her faith in God, too, until she finally struck bottom, hard. With her

Second Chance Drifter

support network shredded, she had turned to the only one who could heal her despair: Jesus.

There were about 30 people in the Assemblies of God fellowship that Wednesday night, and as I sat with Mama, I recalled my childhood days holding Cassie's hand, slowly making our way to the podium, our innocent voices filling that sanctuary.

Innocence — that was a lifetime ago, I remembered thinking. Sorrow over my lifestyle had percolated throughout the pastor's sermon. I wrestled with immorality, addictions and pride, and I broke down when the preacher spoke about the prodigal son and how his loving father welcomed him home. I walked to the front of the church and asked Jesus to heal my train-wreck-of-a-life.

"Jesus, I asked you to save me when I was a kid, and I don't know how it all happens, but I need you now. I don't want these tore-up emotions anymore." It was like a gentle, cleansing wind cleared my drug-clouded mind. Mama was crying with me, and in the next few weeks, I seized the relationship with God that I had yearned for my whole life. I devoured the Bible like a starving man, and it wasn't enough to speak my prayers. I wrote them down on paper, thankful, and sometimes filled with regret.

"Lord, I am so sorry for the time I have wasted."

A gentle, powerful voice overpowered every thought in my mind. "I have made time for you."

My Creator was giving me a second chance! I rolled out the old futon in Mama's living room, and new purpose electrified me. In the dark, I worshiped

This Could Be You

God as my soul rang with songs of deliverance from an empty life of futile dreams.

But what about my ambition to see my name on a marquee in Nashville, or on a record label? Faintly, in the depths of my being, a vile jukebox still scratched out the song that played over and over: *Barstool Country, it ain't never gonna die.*

***

I slouched at the kitchen table, still bleeding from my mouth, head in my hands. "God save me. Please, God."

I had gambled my eternity to chase celebrity, and now all that remained in my future was sad lyrics of regret: *meth, then sorrow, meth, then sorrow.* Who was I kidding? I had stretched God's patience to the limit.

The ringing phone barely pierced my daydreams, and when I answered, I hardly believed what I was hearing. "We're moving to Washington State, Kevin, and you're welcome to join us." Mama's voice was hopeful.

How many chances did God give a traitor like me, anyway?

Mama and her Godly new husband accepted my offer to drive a moving truck on the 3,000-mile trip west, and at times, it seemed that I breathed pure oxygen while I pondered how God might be orchestrating my rescue. Still, I hid away a baggie of marijuana to help me survive if I couldn't find dope in "Hicksville."

Second Chance Drifter

I had little to fear. Even in the little town of Chehalis, Washington, dope dealers pandered to junkies. In the months ahead, I found work while my family established a Christian home church, and I often stole away to smoke pot when despair overwhelmed me. It seemed a pipe dream that my new surroundings alone would halt my slide toward hell. I was clawing up a rock face, seeing the handholds but lacking the will to climb.

Two Kevins had moved west: Kevin Emerson, beaten and repentant, pleading with God to save him, and Kevin Singer, the proud artist, the junkie. Both had to die so that Jesus could create a completely new man.

Yes, Jesus loves me… the Bible tells me so.

"Kevin, there's someone here to see you." We had lived in Chehalis for three months when Mama seated two strangers in her living room, a nervous looking man and his wife. I glanced at my mother, whose questioning shrug made me uneasy.

"I don't know you, but," the man leaned forward and his face changed to a firm sincerity, "I saw you in your yard the other day as I drove by, and I thought I recognized you from somewhere. Then last night, I had a dream, and you were in it. I think this dream is from God." He adjusted his bulk on the couch and smiled at his wife and back at me. "Is this *weird* to you?"

A sensation like a feather sweeping gently up my bare back made me shiver inside, and I knew that Jesus was visiting my soul. "It makes perfect sense,"

This Could Be You

I said, hesitant to hear the rest of the story, but I had to know.

"It was the gold rush era, when miners dug in the ground searching for riches. I saw a man panning for nuggets — shaking the pan full of dirt, and sloshing it under the cold creek water over and over again, until only gold remained in his pan." Our guest's eyes fixed on mine as he said, "I believe that God is saying to you, 'The shaking of your life is a good thing.' When God is done shaking, what is left will be gold."

I was silent for a few moments while relief flooded my heart. No judgment, no condemnation — I heard *pure* strains of God's mercy playing inside me again!

"I think we should pray," I said quietly.

We all stood up, and the man slowly cupped his hands under my jaw as my body quaked with sobs. I raised my hands in surrender to God, and after several minutes, I came back to my surroundings. I felt like someone had kindled a roaring bonfire in the living room; my clothes were drenched in sweat, and the evil presence that had shadowed me on and off for years had vanished. The toxic, ambitious Kevin Singer was passing away.

After my guests left, I knelt down in my bedroom, exhausted. "God," I said, "I don't want to mess this up. You have done so many good things for me. Forgive me."

I yearned for the former deliverance I owned months ago when I pledged myself to Christ — *then* my addictions had vanished. Drugs had replaced

Second Chance Drifter

Jesus as my "comforter" and now, even after my renewed commitment to him, I wrestled daily with my old addiction. But God was equipping me for a clean break. I immediately had the gumption to throw away my Marlboroughs and chewing tobacco, and whenever I lit up a joint in a dark corner, a sense of doom swept through me. A morbid depression weighed upon me, instead of the old dope tranquility I counted on.

I was driving stoned one day when I believe God spoke to me about the weed stuffed in my pocket. "Throw it out the window."

"Hey, man, is that *you* talking to me?" In my condition, I worried that I could be hearing from my evil groupies again.

"Kevin, I can talk to you whenever I want — if you are stoned, or high on meth, or asleep, or anytime. And would the devil be telling you to toss your stuff?"

"But I *am* stoned."

"You're intoxicated, but it'll wear off."

And this surreal exchange with my Creator somehow helped seal my decision to forsake drugs, once and for all.

"Why don't you come to church with me, Kevin?" Michael was like me, an idea man, and we hit it off immediately while lifting weights together at Thorbecke's gym in Chehalis.

I accepted his invitation, and I felt such relief knowing that the "old Kevin" would never show up again to scope out the "church hypocrites." Destiny Christian Center seemed really peculiar. Young men

This Could Be You

and women my age dressed casually, and many shared the same struggles with addictions and immorality as I had, and now their hearts were *clean*. I felt truly comfortable around them and soaked up the word of God like a sponge as Pastor Bill preached. In the coming months, fellowship with these likeminded believers surpassed any social fulfillment that I had ever experienced — I was *home*. That was nearly five years ago.

I'm still swinging a hammer, but my real job is at Destiny with those who work shoulder to shoulder with me, accepting and loving misfits (like myself) that I bring in for Jesus to salvage. And I still use my gift to connect with an audience — leading worship on Sunday mornings or in youth ministry — but no longer to gin up anguish to feed my ambition. I want people to know the Savior who replaced my ambitions like strings on a derelict guitar and gave me new music, the one who saved me from addictions and despair.

Each week I scan hundreds of faces in our "Clothes and Loaves" ministry, as the Holy Spirit points out those individuals bruised by hard times: a youth whose eyes scream out for healing from addictions; a crying baby who senses emotional wounds in her teenage mother; a homeless man emptied of hope. My team members and I flow among these people with genuine, healing encouragement, without judging or targeting them for "Christianity." Jesus does that. We just feed em' and love em' — and listen to their heartbreaks. And often, I weep inside as I tell them about a guy I know who believed he

Second Chance Drifter

had fallen past saving — over and over — and how Jesus rescued him, once and for all.

Conclusion

Well, what do you think? Winners? Maybe not in the way we would think because there was really no way to determine their victory. What was the score? Who was the opponent?

I gave my life to Christ when I was a competitive little 9 year old. A song, "Victory In Jesus," was sung at the conclusion of the service. The song impressed upon my young spirit that I could get a victory if I gave my life to Jesus. I went forward and knelt on a sawdust floor and made the same decision that those mentioned in this book did, and I became a winner that night.

The key is found in what my reward or prize was — what exactly did I win? Well, I think it was really a win-win situation because I won by accepting a friend that would be with me forever, and my friend was committed to making my life the very best it could be. I also win because my friend has guaranteed me eternal life with him in heaven. I win in this life because I have found the source of true, abundant life, and I win in the life to come, also. What a deal!

In my introduction, I alluded to the fact that this victory was free. It is. Jesus, my friend, already paid the price, that of dying on the cross for me. The Bible says that he became sin for me, for us. Therefore, when he went to the cross, he had on his shoulders all of our sins and then took the punishment for

This Could Be You

them that we should receive. Since the price is paid, the victory is ours. We win. Period. It's that simple.

If you want to have a life that is better than you could ever imagine — be a winner — then all you have to do is exactly the same as those in this book did. Ask Jesus to forgive you of your sins. You can do it right where you are, or you can call me at 360-736-6443, and I'll be glad to help you walk through it. How about a prayer to help you? Pray this prayer and then call me, okay?

"Dear Jesus, I don't totally understand all of this, but I ask you right now to forgive me for my sins. Thanks for paying the price for me on the cross and dying for my sins. I want you to come into my life and make the changes that these people in this book experienced. I surrender my life to you. Thank you for forgiving me, giving me new life and promising me eternal life in heaven with you. In Jesus' name, Amen."

Congratulations! You are a winner! You are on your way to the most thrilling life one could ever experience. Here are some quick steps:

1. Find a local church. If you do not know of any, call me, and I'll help you out.

2. Get a Bible and begin to read it every day. Start with the book called Psalms or Mark.

3. Call someone you know who is a Christian, and let them know that you are a winner. If you do not know any, again, hey, call me!

4. Begin to pray… all the time… it's simple — just talk to God the way you talk to a friend.

The people in this book attend Destiny Christian

Conclusion

Center in Centralia and will be more than happy to share further with you and answer any of your questions. I am looking forward to meeting you — I love meeting other winners!

God bless you — way to go! Another winner for Jesus!

Bill G. Bates
Pastor

We would love for you to join us on Sunday morning! We gather at 419 N. Tower Rd. Centralia, WA 98531 at 10:30 am.

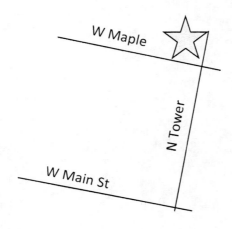

Please call us at 360.736.6443 for directions or contact us at www.lifeatdestiny.com.

For more information on reaching your city with stories from your church, please contact Good Catch Publishing at www.goodcatchpublishing.com

Good Catch Publishing